FUNDAMENTALS OF AIRCRAFT

AND FLYING CONCEPTS

HOW AIRCRAFT FLY AND ITS ENVIRONMENT

Dr. J V Muruga Lal Jeyan

Ms. Jyothi N T

ink Scribe

ink

Fundamentals Of Aircraft And Flying Concepts

Publisher: Inkscribe Publishing Pvt. Ltd

ISBN Number: 978-1-966421-91-7

DEDICATION

I love you all and miss you all beyond words. May the lord Shiva grant you all a truthful globe. First and foremost, I thank Ms Jyothi NT for letting me breathe to write this book through. I dedicate this to my Research students for unwavering support, encouragements and patience through this process.

— Dr. Lal

This book is dedicated to my mother , Thulasi – who are the constant source of inspiration for me and and my dear research supervisor Dr lal my well wisher. -Whose constant encouragement and blessings filled with love I cannot repay.

— Ms. Jyothi NT

CONTENTS

ACKNOWLEDGMENTS

I would like to express my special appreciation and thanks to my advisor Professor Dr. M. Senthil Kumar, you have been a tremendous mentor for me. I would like to thank Ms. Jyothi NT President LIPS research for encouraging my explore and for forcing me to Bounce back stronger. Your advice my career have been priceless. A special thanks to my family. Words cannot express how grateful I am to my mother, father and family for all of the sacrifices that you've made on my behalf. And my favourite friends Your prayer for me was what sustained me thus far

— Dr. Lal

First of all , I offer my reverences to the Almighty God for the wisdom he bestowed upon me ,the strength , peace of my mind for completion of this book and my parent's who always stood by my side , encouraged me and blessed me with love. The man who groomed my efforts is none other than- Dr. J.V Muruga Lal Jeyan. I feel highly privileged to express my sincere regards and gratitude to him for his dynamic leadership, expert supervision and valuable suggestions. He not only motivated me but also guided me with his skilled knowledge whenever I approached him. The present accomplishment would not have seen the light of the day if I had not received the unstinted cooperation of my grandparents, and all family members..

— Ms. Jyothi NT

CHAPTER 1

INTRODUCTION TO ATMOSPHERE

INTRODUCTION

International Standard Atmosphere, solar system, Kepler's Laws, Asteroids and Meteoroids, Early air vehicles and classifications, concept of biplanes and monoplanes, Mach number regions of sound , flow regions and parameters, basic of hypervelocity flow and basic shock layer, escape velocity.

INTERNATIONAL STANDARD ATMOSPHERE

It is important to understand the definition of various altitudes that are usually used to analyze/compare the performance of flying vehicles in standard atmosphere. The gravitational force experienced by any aircraft varies with altitude. Also, an aircraft experiences variation in aerodynamic forces with altitude. This is simply because of the fact that the atmospheric properties viz; Pressure, density and Temperature (P; ϱ; T) also changes with altitude. Aerodynamic forces are strong function of these atmospheric properties (P; ϱ; T). It is a necessity to specify the altitude that will help in postulating gravitational and aerodynamic forces explicitly.

Standard atmosphere is defined in order to relate flight tests, wind tunnel tests general airplane design and performance to a common reference.

1. Absolute altitude (h_a) : The altitude as measured from the center of the earth.

2. Geometric altitude (h_g) : The altitude as measured from the mean sea level.

3. Geo-potential altitude (h) : The geometric altitude corrected for the gravity variation.

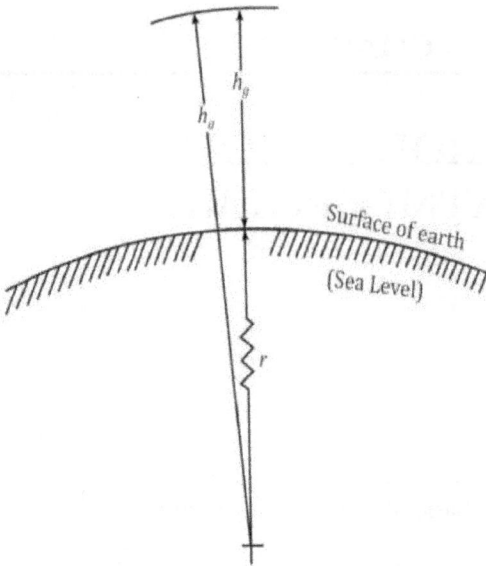

Schematic diagram representing geometric altitude and absolute altitude

The atmosphere is divided into 4 major layers according to the changes in temperature :

- Thermosphere 80 KM & up
- Mesosphere 50 to 80 KM
- Stratosphere 12 to 50 KM
- Troposphere 0 to 12 KM

a) Ionosphere
b) Exosphere

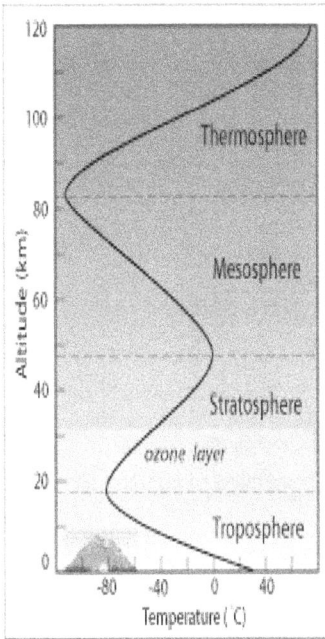

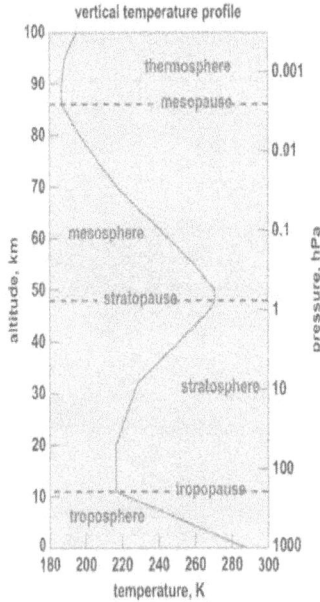

Troposphere (0 – 12 km)

- Contains 75 % of the total gas in the atmosphere
- This layer is where we live and change in weather occurs
- The temperature drops about 6.5° C for every one kilometer
- The warmest temperatures in the troposphere are near the surface with the coldest temperatures being at the top of the troposphere.
- Although the sun light comes from the top to the bottom of the atmosphere, the troposphere is primarily heated from the bottom.
- because the earth surface is much better at absorbing wide range of solar radiation as compared to the air.
- The surface is warmed by the sun and then this energy is distributed upwards into the troposphere through a mixing of the air.
- Since the earth's surface is the primary heat source, temperatures will be warmest at the surface and decrease away from the surface.
- Located at the top of the troposphere.
- Temperature maintain constant at this instant.
- The layer separate the Troposphere from the stratosphere.

Stratosphere (12 to 50 Km)

- It is the lower part of stratopause.

- The increase of temperature with altitude, is a result of the absorption of the Sun's ultraviolet radiation by ozone.
- This is in contrast to the troposphere, near the Earth's surface, where temperatures decreases with altitude.
- After the tropopause , marks where this temperature inversion begins.

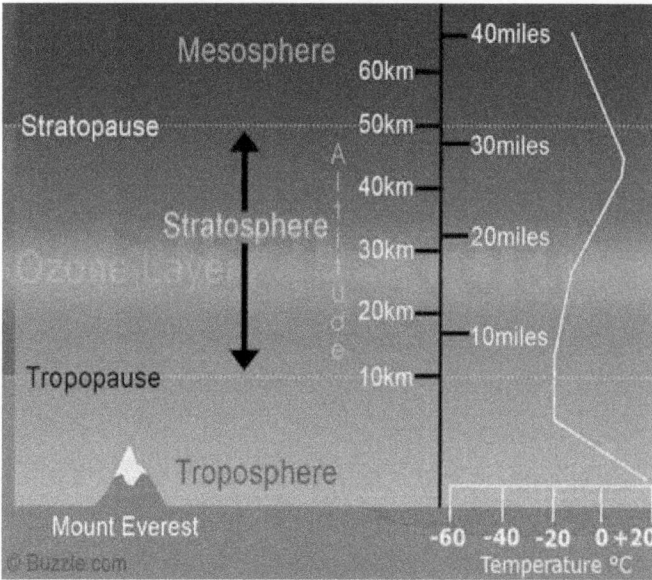

Mesosphere (50 to 80 Km)

- The mesosphere, temperature decreases as the altitude increases.
- The upper boundary of the mesosphere is the mesopause
- Which can be the coldest naturally occurring place on Earth with temperatures below 130 K (-143 °C).
- The exact upper and lower boundaries of the mesosphere vary with latitude and with season
- But the lower boundary of the mesosphere is usually located at heights of about 50 kilometers
- This layer protects earth from meteoroids

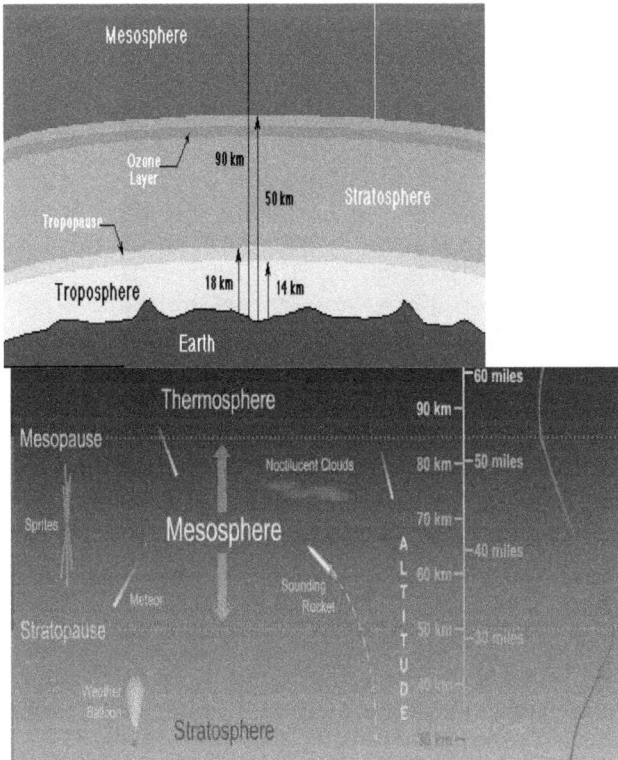

Thermosphere (80 Km & up)

- The air is very thin Thermosphere means heat sphere
- The temperature is very high in the layer
- UV radiation turns in to heat
- Temperature often reaches 2000°C
- Ionosphere
- Exosphere
- An aurora, sometimes referred to as a polar light, is a natural light display in the sky, largely seen in the high latitude regions.

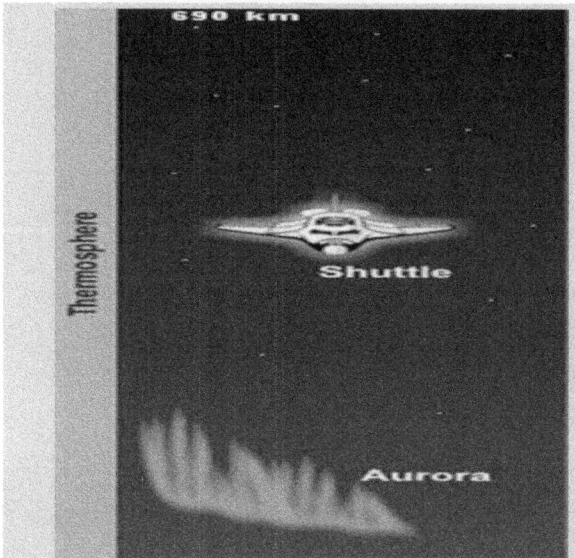

Magnetosphere – the area around the earth that extends beyond atmosphere

SOLAR SYSTEM

The Solar System is the name given to the Sun and its family of planets. This family of planet consists of eight planets and a belt of minor planets or asteroids. They all move in elliptical orbits around the sun due to its force of gravitational attraction.

The eight major planets in the Solar System are:

- Mercury
- Venus
- Earth
- Mars
- Jupiter
- Saturn
- Uranus
- Neptune

Pluto was considered to be the ninth planet until 2006 when it was reclassified as a dwarf planet. It has an orbit more common with asteroids rather than the other planets and astronomers suspect that it might once have been a moon of Neptune.

Astronomers have divided the eight major planets into two groups: terrestrial and Jovian.

Terrestrial Planets

The terrestrial planets are Mercury, Venus, Earth and Mars and are made up mostly of Iron and silicate rocks and lie closer to the Sun.

Jovian Planets

The Jovian planets are Jupiter, Saturn, Uranus and Neptune and are made up mostly of Hydrogen and Helium. Because of their gaseous composition they are also referred to as the Gas Giants. The Jovian planets are the larger more massive planets with strong magnetic fields and they rotate more rapidly about their axes. Unmanned space probes have shown the Jovian planets have ring systems with moons orbiting them.

The Sun

The sun lies in the centre of the Solar System. It is a yellow dwarf star. It has a surface temperature of approximately 6000°C. Its diameter is about 865,000 miles approximately 109 times the diameter of the Earth. By mass the sun is made up of 71% Hydrogen, 28% Helium and the remaining 1% mass comprising heavier atoms such as Carbon, Nitrogen, Oxygen, Silicon and Iron. The sun contains 99% of the Solar Systems mass. It has no fixed surface and the temperature is too high for the matter to exist as a solid or a liquid. Due to this different parts of the sun rotate at different rates. The parts of the surface near the equator complete a rotation in 25 Earth days, whereas the parts near the pole take 36 days.

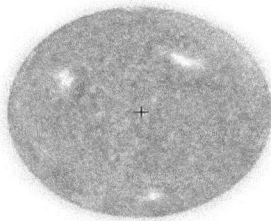

Mercury

Mercury is the smallest of the eight planets in the solar system. It is the planet with the closet orbit to the sun. Its orbit lies between the sun and the orbit of Venus and it has no known moons. Mercury has a diameter of approximately 3000 miles. It is made up of a high percentage of metal making it the densest planet in the solar system. It takes Mercury 88 Earth days to orbit the sun. The fast orbit is offset by the planets slow spin. It takes Mercury 59 Earth days to complete one rotation about its axis.

0.1º

Venus

Venus is the second planet from the sun. Its orbit lies between the orbits of Mercury and Earth and has no known moons. It is the closest planet to the Earth and after the moon is the most brilliant natural object in the night sky. Venus has a diameter of approximately 12,100 km making it slightly smaller than Earth (Earth's diameter is approximately 12,750 km). Although further away from the sun than Mercury, Venus is the hottest planet in the solar system. This is because it has a very large atmosphere made up mostly of Carbon Dioxide. This thick, dense atmosphere traps the heat radiated from the planet's surface and the sun (greenhouse effect) making the average temperature on Venus about 460°Celsius. Venus spins about its axis very slowly taking 243 Earth days to complete one rotation,

177º

which is the length of a day on Venus. It completes one orbital revolution of the sun in 225 Earth days making Venus the only planet where a day is longer than a year. Venus rotates about its axis in a retrograde motion i.e. in a direction opposite to the other planets. Venus and Neptune are the only planets which rotate counter clockwise while the other 6 planets rotate clockwise.

Earth

Earth is the third planet from the sun. It is the only planet that hosts all known life. Its orbit lies between Venus and Mars and has one moon. The Earth has a diameter at the equator of 12,756km. It spins about its axis once every 24 hours (1 Earth day) and takes 365.256 days to orbit the sun. The Earth's atmosphere is made up of 78% Nitrogen, 21% Oxygen and the remaining 1% consists of other gases such as Argon, Carbon Dioxide, Methane and Hydrogen.

23°

Mars

Mars is the fourth planet from the sun. The orbit of Mars lies between Earth's orbit and Jupiter's orbit. Between Mars and Jupiter lies the main asteroid belt. Mars has two small moons called Phobos and Deimos. Mars is the second smallest planet in the solar system. Its diameter at the equator is approximately 6,800km. It takes Mars 687 days to complete one revolution of the sun. Thus, one year on Mars is equivalent to almost 2 Earth years. Mars is called the red planet due to the reddish brown Iron Oxide on its surface. Its atmosphere is made up mostly of Carbon Dioxide, however the atmosphere is very thin making the average temperature on the surface average about -70°Celsius.

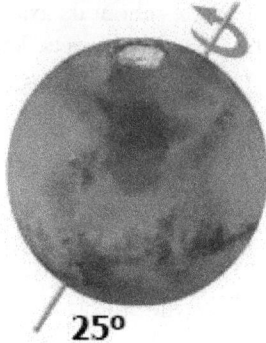

25°

Jupiter

Jupiter is the fifth planet from the sun. It is the largest planet in the solar system with a diameter at the equator of approximately 143000km. More than 1300 Earths can fit inside Jupiter. Jupiter holds more matter than all the other planets in the solar system. Its strong gravitational pull is accountable for the many moons that orbit the planet. To date more than 60 known moons orbit Jupiter. It completes one rotation in 9hours 55 minutes, which is the length of a day on Jupiter. It takes about 11.9 earth years to orbit the sun. Jupiter has no solid surface. It is composed mainly of Hydrogen and Helium. The large pressures in the planets interior account for Hydrogen and Helium in the liquid form surrounded by a gaseous atmosphere. The Great Red Spot is a huge oval shape storm

3°

system in the planets southern hemisphere.

Saturn

Saturn is the sixth planet from the sun. After Jupiter it is the second largest planet in the solar system. Its diameter at the equator is approximately 75000 miles (120,500 km). Saturn's orbit lies between Jupiter and Uranus and it takes about 30 Earth years to complete one revolution around the sun. It rotates about its axis in 10.8 hours, which is the length of a day on Saturn. Saturn like Jupiter is one of the gas giants and is composed mostly of Hydrogen and some Helium. Saturn's most famous feature is its ring system. This is made up of hundreds of thousands of individual rings held in orbit by the pull of Saturn's gravity. The rings are made up of countless ice chunks and dust particles. In addition to the ring system there are more

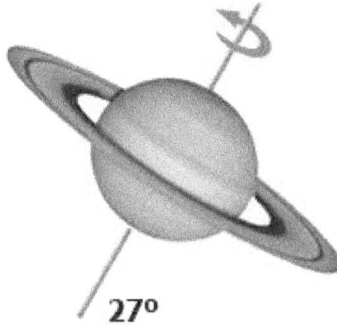

27°

than 50 known moons that orbit Saturn.

Uranus
Uranus is the seventh planet from the sun. Its diameter at the equator is about 32000 miles (51500 km) making it the third largest planet in the solar system. It takes Uranus 84 Earth days to complete one trip around the sun. Uranus completes one rotation on its axis in approximately 17 Earth hours, which is a length of a day on Uranus. Uranus is different to the other planets in that its rotation axis lies nearly to its side as it goes around the sun. Like Venus it rotates about its axis in a retrograde motion. Scientists think that this alignment may have been caused by violent collisions with other bodies early in its history. Uranus has a liquid interior due to very high temperatures and pressures inside the planet. It is made up of the melted ices of water, methane and ammonia, along with molten rock and metals and small amounts of Hydrogen and Helium. Uranus has a massive atmosphere made up of approximately 75% Hydrogen and 25% Helium with small amounts of methane, water and ammonia. Uranus has a system of about 12 narrow rings; the rings are made up of countless particles orbiting the planet. Uranus has 5 major moons and more than 20 smaller ones.

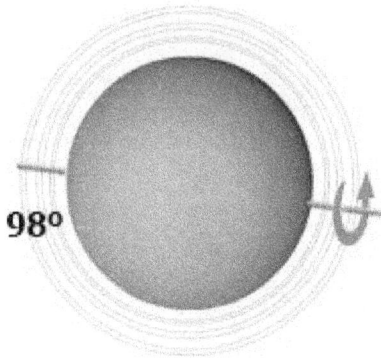

98°

Neptune

Neptune is the eight and farthest most planet from the sun and cannot been seen by the unaided eye. It has a diameter of approximately 31000 miles (50000 km). It takes Neptune 146 Earth years to orbit the sun. Neptune takes 16 hours to complete one rotation about its axis, which is a length of a day on Neptune. Like the other gas giants Neptune has a massive atmosphere made mostly of Hydrogen with some Helium and about 2% of Methane. It is the Methane in Neptune's atmosphere that makes it appear bluish in color. The interior is similar to Uranus being made up of melted ices of water, Methane and Ammonia, along with molten rocks and metals. Neptune has 6 narrow rings composed of dust size particles orbiting the planet. Neptune has 13 known moons.

Pluto

Pluto was discovered in 1930 and was considered the ninth planet of the solar system up until 2006 when it was classified as a dwarf planet. This

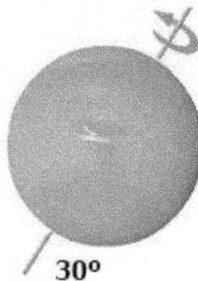

30°

was due to many other objects of a similar size to Pluto being discovered in a region where it lies called the Kuiper belt. So, rather increase the number of planets each time a new object was discovered the definition of planets was redefined to exclude objects such as Pluto and a new category called dwarf planets was designated for Pluto. Pluto has a diameter of about 1500 miles (2400 km). It takes Pluto 248 years to complete a trip around the sun, which is the length of a year on Pluto. It completes one rotation about its axis in 6.4 Earth days. Its atmosphere is composed of Nitrogen with small amounts of Methane and Carbon Monoxide. Its interiors is thought to be made of rock and ice. Because of its great distance from the sun the surface temperature on Pluto is extremely cold. Pluto has one known moon.

KEPLER'S LAWS
Kepler's First Law

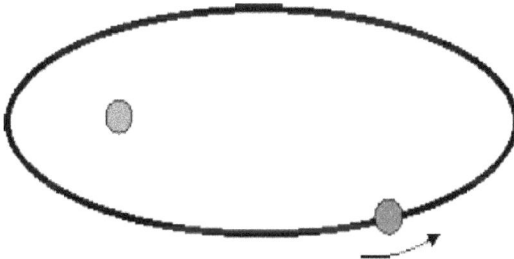

Illustration 2: The Earth orbiting around the Sun.

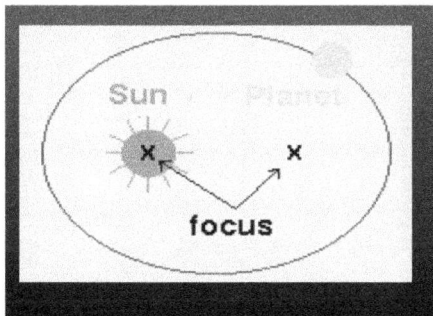

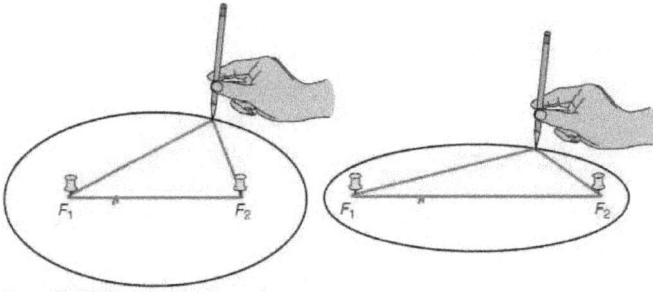

Kepler's Second Law

Kepler's Second Law is based on the speed of the object as it orbits.
It states that in their orbits around the sun, the planets sweep out equal areas in equal times.

Kepler's Third Law

The big mathematical accomplishment for Kepler is in his Third Law, where he relates the radius of an orbit to it's period of orbit (the time it takes to complete one orbit).
The squares of the times to complete one orbit are proportional to the cubes of the average distances from the Sun.

$$K = \frac{T^2}{r^3}$$

T = period (in any unit, usually seconds)
r = radius (in any unit, usually metres)
K = Kepler's Constant

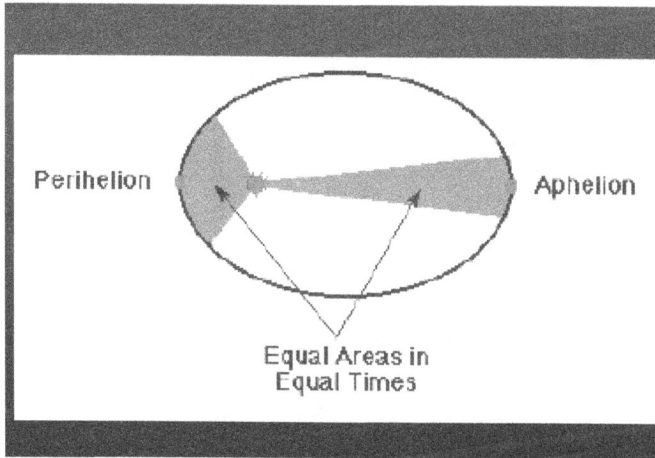

Perihelion

Aphelion

Equal Areas in
Equal Times

ASTEROIDS AND METEOROIDS
Asteroid
An asteroid is a celestial body - composed of rock, metal or a mixture of both - that is orbiting the Sun. Most of them are in the asteroid belt between Mars and Jupiter. Even though there are millions of asteroids with sizes up to more than 500 km (like Pallas and Vesta) they are of no danger to the planet Earth. The biggest body in the asteroid belt - Ceres - is officially not called an asteroid anymore but a dwarf planet. If you try to envision the asteroid belt don't get fooled by some science fiction films: travelling around in the asteroid belt with your spacecraft doesn't require constant steering in order to avoid crashes with asteroids. The scale of the solar system is so immense that even inside the asteroid belt the average distance between two asteroids is above one million km - or three times the distance between Earth and the Moon.

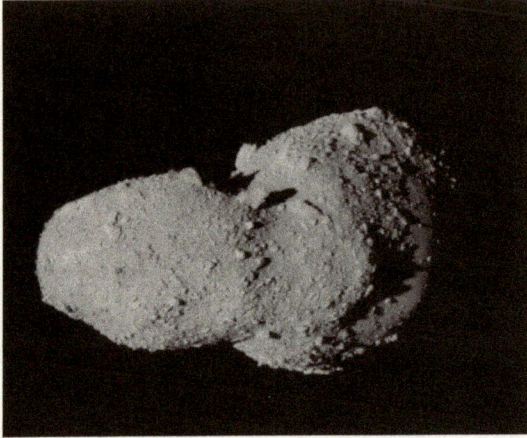

Meteoroids and meteors

Generally speaking, meteoroids are all the smaller objects in orbit around the Sun. Most of them originate from comets that lose gas and dust when they approach the Sun. Other meteoroids are basically small asteroids. There is no exact diameter that distinguishes an asteroid from a meteoroid. Wikipedia states 10 meters; other trustworthy sites call anything smaller than 1 km a meteoroid. Anyhow, the vast majority of all meteoroids are just a few millimeters and less in size. The smallest and by far the most numerous ones have sizes of small dust particles and are called micrometeoroids; they do not leave any visible trace behind when they enter the Earth's atmosphere.

The ones about the size of a pebble leave behind a flash of light when they completely vaporize. Most people call this flash a "shooting star" or a "falling star", but more accurately spoken this is a meteor. A meteor is the light that you can see when a small meteoroid enters the Earth's atmosphere. This normally happens with speeds between 11 and 73 km/s and at altitudes of about 75-120 km. Under a clear sky an observer can see 5 to 10 meteors per hour, especially after midnight when the Earth has rotated so far that the observer's part of the sky is positioned in the direction of the Earth's motion around the Sun. During so called meteor showers the rate of observable meteors per hour can increase significantly. Meteor showers are caused when the Earth crosses higher than usual concentrations of particles that are themselves in an eccentric orbit around the Sun. Since the orbit of these particles is fixed, we encounter this stream every year at the same time - just its density cannot be foreseen. This sometimes leads to sparse meteor showers and sometimes very intense meteor showers with more than 1000 meteors per hour, also called meteor outbursts or meteor storms. The meteors we see can be debris from a comet (> 90% of all meteors we see) or an asteroid. The most famous meteor showers are the Perseids in mid-August (caused by Comet 109P/Swift-Tuttle) and the Leonids (mid-November). The meteors during these meteor showers almost all emerge from the same section of the sky; indeed the meteor showers are named for the constellations from which the meteors appear to originate.

Smaller meteoroids will be heated by adiabatic compression until the point when they completely disintegrate. However, the light emission we observe is mainly caused by interactions between evaporated and detached components of the fast moving meteoroid and air molecules. Both the meteoroid atoms and the air molecules ionize during this encounter. When the free electrons recombine with the ionized atoms in the tail of the meteoroid they emit the light that we can observe. The light track can have a length of up to several tens of kilometres and an initial diameter of a few metres. The colour of the meteor is an indicator of the material of the meteoroid; e.g., a yellow colour is caused by iron, a blue-green colour by copper and a red colour by silicate material.

A meteor that is larger and brighter than normal is called a fireball;

brighter than the brightest planet in our night sky (Venus). If these fireballs also break apart or explode during their atmospheric flight - sometimes accompanied by considerable audible sounds - they are called a bolide.

Comets

Comets are asteroid-like objects which are composed of ice, dust and rocky particles; that's why they are also called 'dirty snowballs'. The sizes of their nuclei vary between a few hundred metres to tens of kilometres in diameter; their visible tails can extend to above 150 million km in length. They originate from outside Neptune's orbit and - like many asteroids and meteoroids - are unmodified remnants of the formation of our solar system about 4.568 billion years ago. When comets approach the Sun the solar radiation and solar winds cause particles to sublimate and detach from the comet, forming a tail of particles which often makes them visible in the night sky even to the naked eye. We say 'sublimate' (a direct phase transition from the solid to the gas phase) since with zero pressure in space, water will not exist in the liquid phase. Anyhow, below its surface there can also be reservoirs of liquid water which can vaporize and feed jets of water vapor.

EARLY AIR VEHICLES AND CLASSIFICATIONS
History of flight

In the Vedas and later Indian literature has detailed "vimanas" of various shapes and sizes:

The word Vimana comprises of Vi, "the sky" and Mana,, "measure" = Vimana Indian legends have many concepts of Vimana.
In the Vedas: the Sun, Indra & several other Vedic deities are transported by flying wheeled chariots
•Pulled by animals, usually horses (but the Vedic god Pusan's chariot is pulled by goats).
•The **"agnihotra vimana"** with two engines. (Agni means fire in Sanskrit.)
•The **"gaja vimana"** with more engines. (Gaja means elephant in Sanskrit.)
•Other types named after the kingfisher, ibis, and other animals.
Pushpaka Vimanas-The first flying airplane on earth!!???
- Kubera, the Lord of Wealth, had an air plane according to Valmiki Ramayana
- That was the earliest plane that the human beings knew
- Ravana confiscated it from Kubera. After death Vibhshana, brother of Ravana, presented the air plane to Lord Rama. This was the fastest plane in those days.

- We know the secret of Lord Rama's plane (Pushpaka Vimana). Ram flew the plane by THOUGHT POWER!
- It took ONE DAY to cover the distance between Sri Lanka and Ayodhya in Uttar Pradesh of India
- Like modern planes it was in silvery white in colour (shiny)(solar cells)
- The distance between the two cities was approximately 3000 miles.
- plane flew low (unlike modern jet planes) only during day time
- "Have a safe journey reach before sun set". Vibhishana said the same to Rama.
- Refuses to believe Valmiki, "should at least give the credit of First Science Fiction writer in the world to Valmiki! "

The Flight route of Rama

1. Lanka (Ceylon)	13. Pamavati off Nasik
2. Nikumbhila sacrifice-altar	14. Agastyasrama, S. E. of Nasik
3. Hiranyagarbha Mt. Munnar Bay	15. Sarabhangasrama (Jubbelpore)
4. Setubandha	16. Citrakuta hill off Banda
5. Ramesvaram	17. River Jamuna
6. Malyavan hill	18. Bharadwajasrama (Colonelganj)
7. Kiskndhya	19. Srngaverapura, 18 miles N. W,
8. Rsyamukha Mt.	of Allahabad
9. Pampa Lake	20. River Ganges
10. Tungabhadra river	21. Nandigrama (Nandagaon, Oudh)
11. Godavari river	
12. Janasthana (Aurangavad)	

www.mallstuffs.com

Chinese kite flying

- It was invented in china possibly by 5th century BC by mozi and luban
- Few are designed in early days with whistles to make musical sounds
- After it introduced in india , further evolved in to kite fight , where abrasive liners are used to cut other kites
- In 6th century man carrying kites are used for both civil and military purpose

- Even some time enforced as punishment

Balloon flight
- 1783 was the fantastic year for ballooning aviation
- Between june 4 and December 1 five aviation programed in France
- On June 4th the Montgolfier brothers demonstrated their unmaned hot air balloon at - france
- On 27th aug Jacques charkes & Robert brothers launched the worlds first unmaned hydrogen filled balloon at paris
- On 19th October the Montgolfier launched the first manned flight , balloon with humans on board at folie titon in paries
- There is evidence that the chieses also solved the problems of aerial navigation using balloons 18th century

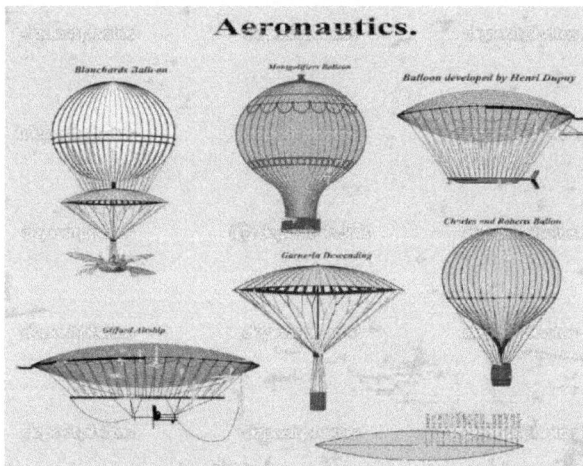

Aeronautics.

Ornithopters (Leonardo da vinci - 1485)
- Leonardo - has developed more than 100 drawings on theories of flight
- It was design created to show how man can fly
- It's a aircraft heavier than air which flies like a bird
- The special features that lies in the wing which generate both lift and thrust

Design and method of an ornithopter
- Aerodynamic machine with 2 working cycle (up & down stroke)
- In up stroke air flow hits the wing upper surface and at down stroke hits at bottom
- Lift generated during the down ward stroke
- Thrust is generated along the whole wing span during stroke motion it works similar to a propeller blade

Early airplane by wright brothers
- This brothers build series of gliders and kite with the concept of controllability of A/C – 1900 to 1902
- The first glider launched in 1900 it gives only about half the lift what they anticipated
- Their second glider even performed very poorly
- They corrected their testing and calculating procedure with thumb rules
- The third glider with true three axis control they generated was far better than previous
- They flew it more than 100 times successfully in 1902
- The brothers not only made a powered aircraft they give advancement in science of aeronautical engineering

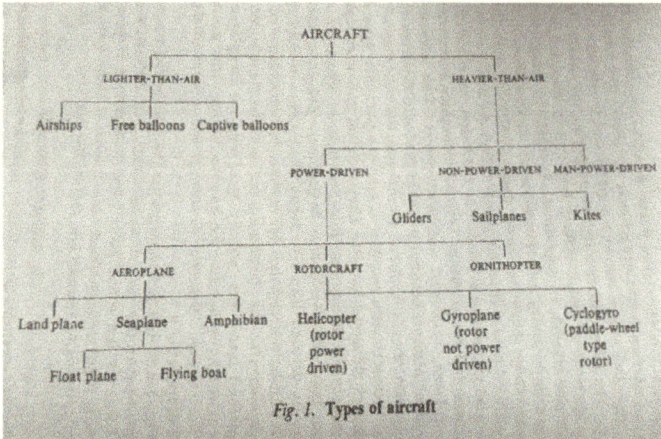

AIRCRAFT

LIGHTER-THAN-AIR — HEAVIER-THAN-AIR

Airships   Free balloons   Captive balloons

POWER-DRIVEN   NON-POWER-DRIVEN   MAN-POWER-DRIVEN

Gliders   Sailplanes   Kites

AEROPLANE   ROTORCRAFT   ORNITHOPTER

Land plane   Seaplane   Amphibian   Helicopter (rotor power driven)   Gyroplane (rotor not power driven)   Cyclogyro (paddle-wheel type rotor)

Float plane   Flying boat

Fig. 1. **Types of aircraft**

Rotorcraft

Types
1. Helicopter
2. Cyclogyro / cyclocopter
3. Autogyro
4. Gyrodyne / gyro plane
5. Rotorkite

- Known as rotary wing aircraft
- Lift generated by rotary wings (no fixed wing)
- Several rotor wings mounted on a single rotor mast
- In some cases one or more rotor assembly will be mounted for better list and maneuvering some design includes additional static surfaces for lift, propellers , thrust engines etc.,

Helicopter

- Is a rotor craft whose rotors are driven by a engine through out the flight
- It take off vertically, hover, fly forward , back ward , laterally and land vertically.
- VTOL
- Several configurations are their with one or more rotors.

Cyclogyro / cyclo copter
- Rotorcraft rotor is driven by the engine through out the flight
- The blade rotates about the horizontal axis
- Blade parallel to its camber

Auto gyro / gyro plane / gyro copter / rotor plane

- All the above type utilize an unpowered rotor driven by aerodynamics forces
- Tat rotor will generate lift
- An engine powered propeller will be their to produce thrust

Gyordyne

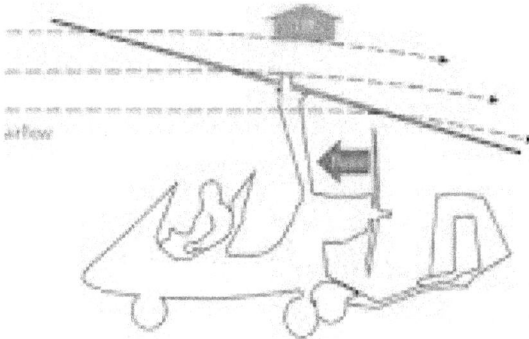

Gyrocopter in autorotation

- VTOL type aircraft Rotor generally driven by engine
- Like a helicopter with anti- torque rotor
- For forward flight one or more propeller mounted on short stub wing
- After level flight thrust being provide by the propellers , the rotor receives less power just to over come profile drag and maintain lift

Rotor kite

- Is an up powered rotary wing aircraft
- The rotor kite has no wing at all
- Being carried and dropped from another aircraft
- Or by towed in to air behind a car or boat

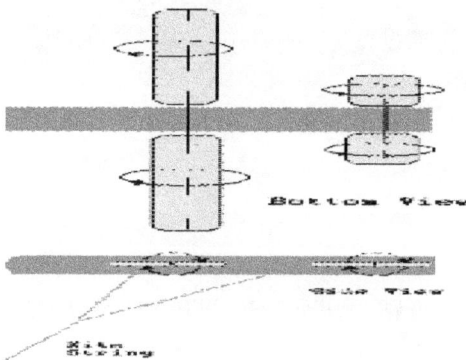

Airships

- Lighter then air aircraft
- Can navigate through air under its own power

- Get lift by large air bags filled with a lifting gas that is less dense than surrounding air
- Rigid construction
- Semi rigid construction
- Non rigid construction

- ***Aerostatic lift*** is the bouyant force acting on a body due to its lesser density than the air environment surrounding it. This force will keep lighter-than-vehicles airborne.
- ***Aerodynamic lift*** acting on a body is the lift force that is generated as a result of velocity of thebody relative to the air environment. This force is useful to keep heavier-than-air vehicles airborne.

CONCEPT OF BIPLANES AND MONOPLANE
Biplane
- A biplane is a fixed wing aircraft with two fixed wings stacked one above other
- The wright flyer used such a biplane arrangement wing concept

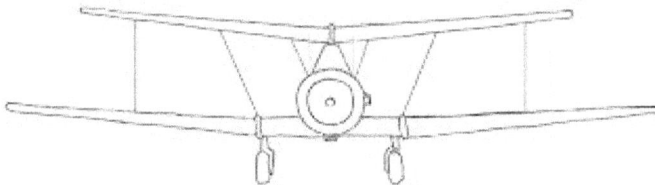

Mono planes

- Is a fixed wing aircraft with a single main wing
- A mono plane has the highest efficiency and lowest drag of any wing configuration
- Its easy and simple construction to build

MONOPLANES

strut-braced wing

cantilever-wing

MACH NUMBER REGIONS OF SOUND

As an aircraft moves through the air, the air molecules near the aircraft are disturbed and move around the aircraft. If the aircraft passes at a low speed, typically less than 250 mph, the density of the air remains constant. But for higher speeds, some of the energy of the aircraft goes into compressing the air and locally changing the density of the air. This compressibility effect alters the amount of resulting force on the aircraft. The effect becomes more important as speed increases. Near and beyond the speed of sound, about 330 m/s or 760 mph, small disturbances in the flow are transmitted to other locations is entropically or with constant entropy. But a sharp disturbance generates a shock wave that affects both the lift and drag of an aircraft.

The ratio of the speed of the aircraft to the speed of sound in the gas determines the magnitude of many of the compressibility effects. Because of the importance of this speed ratio, aerodynamicists have designated it with a special parameter called the **Mach number** in honor of **Ernst Mach**, a late 19th century physicist who studied gas dynamics. The Mach number **M** allows us to define flight regimes in which compressibility effects vary.

1. Subsonic conditions occur for Mach numbers less than one, **M < 1.** For the lowest subsonic conditions, compressibility can be ignored.
2. As the speed of the object approaches the speed of sound, the flight Mach number is nearly equal to one, **M = 1**, and the flow is said to be sonic. At some places on the object, the local speed exceeds the speed of sound. Compressibility effects are most important in transonic flows and lead to the early belief in a **sound barrier**. Flight faster than sound was thought to be impossible. In fact, the sound barrier was only an increase in the drag near sonic conditions because of compressibility effects. Because of the high drag associated with compressibility effects, aircraft do not cruise near Mach 1.
3. Supersonic conditions occur for Mach numbers greater than one, **1 < M < 3**. Compressibility effects are important for supersonic aircraft, and shock waves are generated by the surface of the object. For high supersonic speeds, **3 < M < 5**, aerodynamic heating also becomes very important for aircraft design.
4. For speeds greater than five times the speed of sound, **M > 5**, the flow is said to be hypersonic. At these speeds, some of the energy of the object now goes into exciting the chemical bonds which hold together the nitrogen and oxygen molecules of the air. At hypersonic speeds, the chemistry of the air must be considered when determining forces on the object. The Space Shuttle re-enters the atmosphere at high hypersonic speeds, **M ~ 25**. Under these conditions, the heated air becomes an ionized plasma of gas and the spacecraft must be insulated from the high temperatures.

For supersonic and hypersonic flows, small disturbances are transmitted downstream within a cone. The trigonometric sineof the cone angle **b** is equal to the inverse of the Mach number **M** and the angle is therefore called the Mach angle.

$$\sin(b) = 1 / M$$

There is no upstream influence in a supersonic flow; disturbances are only transmitted downstream.

The Mach number appears as a similarity parameter in many of the equations for compressible flows, shock waves, andexpansions. When wind tunnel testing, you must closely match the Mach number between the experiment and flight conditions. It is completely incorrect to measure a drag coefficient at some low speed (say 200 mph) and apply that drag coefficient at twice the speed of sound (approximately 1400 mph, Mach = 2.0). The compressibility of the air alters the important physics between these two cases.

The Mach number depends on the speed of sound in the gas and the speed of sound depends on the type of gas and the temperature of the gas. The speed of sound varies from planet to planet. On Earth, the atmosphere is composed of mostly diatomic nitrogen and oxygen, and the temperature depends on the altitude in a rather complex way. Scientists and engineers have created a mathematical model of the atmosphere to help them account for the changing effects of temperature with altitude. Mars also has an atmosphere composed of mostly carbon dioxide.

MACH WAVES

Consider an aerodynamic body moving with certain velocity (V) in a still air. When the pressure at the surface of the body is greater than that of the surrounding air, it results an infinitesimal compression wave that moves at speed of sound (a). These disturbances in the medium spread out from the body and become progressively weaker away from the body. If the air has to pass smoothly over the surface of the body, the disturbances must 'warn' the still air, about the approach of the body.
Now analyze two situations:

(a) the body is moving at subsonic speed $(V < a; M < 1)$;

(b) the body is moving at supersonic speed $(V > a; M > 1)$

Case I : During the motion of the body, the sound waves are generated at different time intervals (t).

The distance covered by the sound waves can be represented by the circle of radius $(at, 2at, 3at \ldots\ldots so\, on)$.

During same time intervals (t), the body will cover distances represented by, $Vt, 2Vt, 3Vt \ldots\ldots so\, on$.

At subsonic speeds $(V < a; M < 1)$, the body will always remain inside the family of circular sound waves. In other words, the information is propagated through the sound wave in all directions. Thus, the surrounding still air becomes aware of the presence of the body due to the disturbances induced in the medium. Hence, the flow adjusts itself very much before it approaches the body.

Case II: Consider the case, when the body is moving at supersonic speed $(V > a; M > 1)$.

With a similar manner, the sound waves are represented by circle of radius $(at, 2at, 3at......\text{so on})$ after different time (t) intervals.

By this time, the body would have moved to a different location much faster from its initial position. At any point of time, the location of the body is always outside the family of circles of sound waves. The pressure disturbances created by the body always lags behind the body that created the disturbances. In other words, the information reaches the surrounding air much later because the disturbances cannot overtake the body. Hence, the flow cannot adjust itself when it approaches the body. The nature induces a wave across which the flow properties have to change and this line of disturbance is known as "Mach wave".

These mach waves are initiated when the speed of the body approaches the speed of sound $(V = a; M = 1)$. They become progressively stronger with increase in the Mach number.

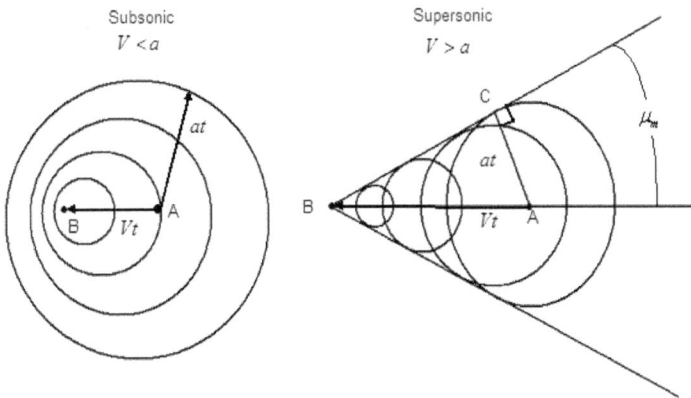

Some silent features of a *Mach wave* are listed below;

- The series of wave fronts form a disturbance envelope given by a straight line which is tangent to the family of circles. It will be seen that all the disturbance waves lie within a cone having a *vertex/apex* at the body at time considered. The locus of all the leading surfaces of the waves of this cone is known as *Mach cone*.

- All disturbances confine inside the Mach cone extending downstream of the moving body is called as *zone of action*. The region outside the Mach cone and extending upstream is known as *zone of silence*. The pressure disturbances are largely concentrated in the neighborhood of the Mach cone that forms the outer limit of the zone of action.

- The half angle of the Mach cone is called as the Mach angle $\left(\mu_m \right)$

$$\sin \mu_m = \frac{at}{Vt} = \frac{a(2t)}{V(2t)} = \frac{a(3t)}{V(3t)} \ldots\ldots = \frac{a}{V} = \frac{1}{M} \Rightarrow \mu_m = \sin^{-1}\left(\frac{1}{M} \right)$$

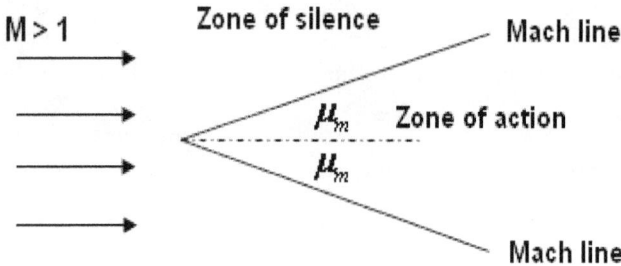

Shock Waves

Let us consider a subsonic and supersonic flow past a body. In both the cases, the body acts as an obstruction to the flow and thus there is a change in energy and momentum of the flow. The changes in flow properties are communicated through pressure waves moving at speed of sound everywhere in the flow field (i.e. both upstream and downstream). If the incoming stream is subsonic i.e. $M_\infty < 1;\ V_\infty < a_\infty$, the sound waves propagate faster than the flow speed and warn the medium about the presence of the body. So, the streamlines approaching the body begin to adjust themselves far upstream and the flow properties change the pattern gradually in the vicinity of the body.

In contrast, when the flow is supersonic, i.e. $M_\infty > 1;\ \ V_\infty > a_\infty$, the sound waves overtake the speed of the body and these weak pressure waves merge themselves ahead of the body leading to compression in the vicinity of the body. In other words, the flow medium gets compressed at a very short distance ahead of the body in a very thin region that may be comparable to the mean free path of the molecules in the medium. Since, these compression waves propagate upstream, so they tend to merge as *shock wave*. Ahead of the shock wave, the flow has no idea of presence of the body and immediately behind the shock; the flow is subsonic

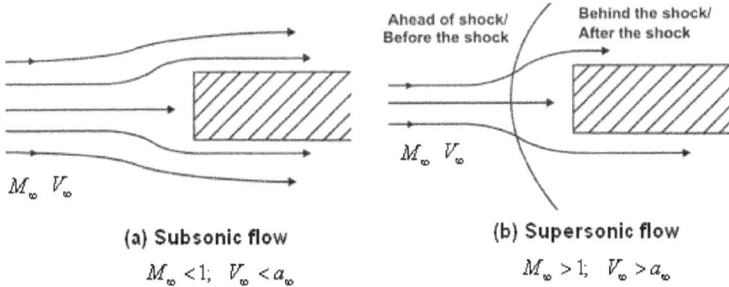

Ahead of shock/
Before the shock

Behind the shock/
After the shock

$M_\infty\ V_\infty$

$M_\infty\ V_\infty$

(a) Subsonic flow

$M_\infty < 1;\ \ V_\infty < a_\infty$

(b) Supersonic flow

$M_\infty > 1;\ \ V_\infty > a_\infty$

FLOW REGIONS AND PARAMETERS

Regime	(Mach number)	(m/s)	General plane characteristics
Subsonic	<0.8	<274	Most often propeller-driven and commercial turbofan aircraft with high aspect-ratio (slender) wings, and rounded features like the nose and leading edges.
Transonic	0.8–1.2	274–412	Transonic aircraft nearly always have swept wings that delay drag-divergence, and often feature designs adhering

			to the principles of the Whitcomb area rule.
Superso nic	1.2–5.0	412– 1,715	Aircraft designed to fly at supersonic speeds show large differences in their aerodynamic design because of the radical differences in the behaviour of fluid flows above Mach 1. Sharp edges, thin airfoil-sections, and all-moving tailplane/canards are common. Modern combat aircraft must compromise in order to maintain low-speed handling; "true" supersonic designs include the F-104 Starfighter and BAC/Aérospatiale Concorde.
Hyperso nic	5.0–10.0	1,715– 3,430	Cooled nickel or titanium skin; highly integrated (due to domination of interference effects: non-linear behaviour means that superposition of results for separate components is invalid), small wings. eg:X-51A Waverider, HyperSoar and WU-14 (DF-ZF).

High-hypersonic	10.0–25.0	3,430–8,575	Thermal control becomes a dominant design consideration. Structure must either be designed to operate hot, or be protected by special silicate tiles or similar. Chemically reacting flow can also cause corrosion of the vehicle's skin, with free-atomic oxygen featuring in very high-speed flows. Examples include the 53T6 *ABM-3 Gazelle* (Mach 17) anti-ballistic missile and DF-41 (Mach 25) intercontinental ballistic missile. Hypersonic designs are often forced into blunt configurations because of the aerodynamic heating rising with a reduced radius of curvature.
Re-entry speeds	>25.0	>8,575	Ablative heat shield; small or no wings; blunt shape.

BASIC OF HYPERVELOCITY FLOW AND BASIC SHOCK LAYER

Hypervelocity is very high velocity, approximately over 3,000 meters per second (6,700 mph, 11,000 km/h, 10,000 ft/s, or Mach 8.8). In particular, hypervelocity is velocity so high that the strength of materials upon impact is very small compared to inertial stresses. Thus, even metals behave like fluids under hypervelocity impact. Extreme hypervelocity results in vaporization of the impactor and target. For structural metals, hypervelocity is generally considered to be over 2,500 m/s (5,600 mph, 9,000 km/h, 8,200 ft/s, or Mach 7.3). Meteorite craters are also examples of hypervelocity impacts.

"Hypervelocity" refers to velocities in the range from a few kilometers per second to some tens of kilometers per second. This is especially relevant in the field of space exploration and military use of space, where hypervelocity impacts (e.g. by space debris or an attacking projectile) can result in anything from minor component degradation to the complete destruction of a spacecraft or missile. The impactor, as well as the surface it hits, can undergo temporary liquefaction. The impact process can generate plasma discharges, which can interfere with spacecraft electronics.

While the definition of hypersonic flow can be quite vague and is generally debatable (especially due to the absence of discontinuity between supersonic and hypersonic flows), a hypersonic flow may be characterized by certain physical phenomena that can no longer be analytically discounted as in supersonic flow. The peculiarity in hypersonic flows are as follows:

- Shock layer
- Aerodynamic heating
- Entropy layer
- Real gas effects
- Low density effects
- Independence of aerodynamic coefficients with Mach number.

Small shock stand-off distance

As a body's Mach number increases, the density behind a bow shock generated by the body also increases, which corresponds to a decrease in volume behind the shock due to conservation of mass. Consequently, the distance between the bow shock and the body decreases at higher Mach numbers.

ESCAPE VELOCITY

Escape velocity is the minimum speed needed for an object to escape from the gravitational influence of a massive body.

The escape velocity from Earth is about 11.186 km/s (6.951 mi/s; 40,270 km/h; 25,020 mph) at the surface. More generally, escape velocity is the speed at which the sum of an object's kinetic energy and its gravitational potential energy is equal to zero an object which has achieved escape velocity is neither on the surface, nor in a closed orbit (of any radius). With escape velocity in a direction pointing away from the ground of a massive body, the object will move away from the body, slowing forever and approaching, but never reaching, zero speed. Once escape velocity is achieved, no further impulse need be applied for it to continue in its escape. In other words, if given escape velocity, the object will move away from the other body, continually slowing, and will asymptotically approach zero speed as the object's distance approaches infinity, never to come back. Speeds higher than escape velocity have a positive speed at infinity. Note that the minimum escape velocity assumes that there is no friction (e.g., atmospheric drag), which would increase the required instantaneous velocity to escape the gravitational influence, and that there will be no future sources of additional velocity (e.g., thrust), which would reduce the required instantaneous velocity.

For a spherically symmetric, massive body such as a star, or planet, the escape velocity for that body, at a given distance, is calculated by the formula

$$v_e = \sqrt{\frac{2GM}{r}}$$

where G is the universal gravitational constant

$(G \approx 6.67 \times 10^{-11}\ \mathrm{m^3 \cdot kg^{-1} \cdot s^{-2}})$,

M the mass of the body to be escaped from, and r the distance from the center of mass of the body to the object. The relationship is independent of the mass of the object escaping the massive body. Conversely, a body that falls under the force of gravitational attraction of mass M, from infinity, starting with zero velocity, will strike the massive object with a velocity equal to its escape velocity given by the same formula.

CHAPTER 2

FUNDAMENTALS OF FLIGHT

Newton's Law for flying, Airfoils and Nomenclature of airfoil, NACA series - Aerodynamic forces, leading and trailing edge high lifts devices, relation between lift , drag and angle of attack curve, Range and Endurance and ceiling, Maneuvers - Aerobatics, dihedral and Anhedral effects in stability

Newton's Law for flying

Law 1: Inertia

The law of inertia has two parts. The first part states that an object at rest will stay at rest unless acted on by a force. A force is a push or a pull. Inertia can be seen when someone pulls a tablecloth out from under dinner plates and the plates stay on the table; the plates stay at rest. Likewise, a plane sitting on the runway will stay at rest until the engine forces it to move.

The second part of Newton's first law states that an object in motion will stay in motion in a straight line, unless acted on by a force. You experience inertia every time a car stops and your body continues to move forward, pulling against the seatbelt and shoulder strap. Were it not for very powerful brakes, a fast-moving plane would continue to roll right off of the runway.

Inertia is a property of mass; massive planes have more inertia than smaller planes. Therefore, massive planes require much more force to speed up or slow down. See inertia for more information.

Law 2: F = ma

The net force acting on an object is equal to the product of its mass and acceleration. A force is a push or pull. If a net force acts on a mass, it will accelerate in the direction of the force. Acceleration is a decrease in speed, an increase in speed, or a change in direction.

Newton's 2nd law states that the acceleration of an object is inversely proportional to its mass. In other words, it is difficult to change the speed of massive objects and it is easier to change the speed of smaller objects. For instance, a full shopping cart is difficult to speed up and slow down. In contrast, if the same amount of force is applied to an empty shopping cart, its speed can be changed more easily.

Example: imagine a motorcycle, a car and a big truck at a stoplight, each with the same horsepower motor. Which vehicle will have a greater acceleration? The motorcycle will have a greater acceleration because its mass is smaller. (Acceleration = Force/Mass) As compared to a massive plane, a small plane is easier to accelerate.

Newton's 2nd law also states that the rate at which an object changes speed is proportional to the force that is exerted. Engines provide thrust and accelerate a plane forward along the runway. If the engines supply a small force, only a small acceleration will result. If a larger force is generated, a larger acceleration will result. Newton's 2nd law can be used to calculate the force required to change the speed of a plane.

Law 3: F = -F

Newton's 3rd Law states that forces always come in equal and opposite pairs. Squeeze your index finger and thumb together. Which pushes with more force? No matter how hard you squeeze, the forces are equal an opposite. Your thumb and finger interaction is an example of an action-reaction pair. If you push on a door, the door pushes back with an equal and opposite force. This is also an action-reaction pair. As you slide a sled down a hill, the frictional forces of the sled are equal and opposite to the frictional forces of the snow. This is another example of an action-reaction pair.

Consider some examples of action-reaction pairs associated with a plane: As a plane sits on the runway, it applies a force on the earth and the earth pushes back with an equal and opposite force. As a plane flies, the force of the air hitting the plane is always equal and opposite to the force of the plane pushing against the air. The force generated by the engine pushes against air while the air pushes back with an equal and opposite force. See Newton's 3rd Law for more information.

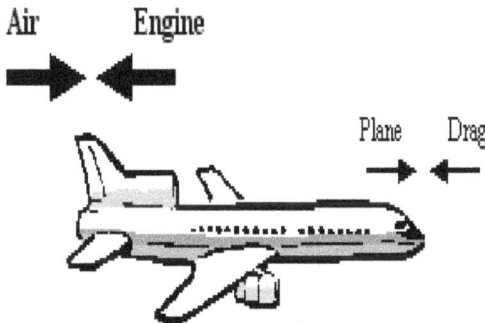

Airfoils and Nomenclature of airfoil

Airfoils are the cross-sectional shapes of wings as defined by , the intersections with the plane parallel to the free stream and normal to the wing plane.

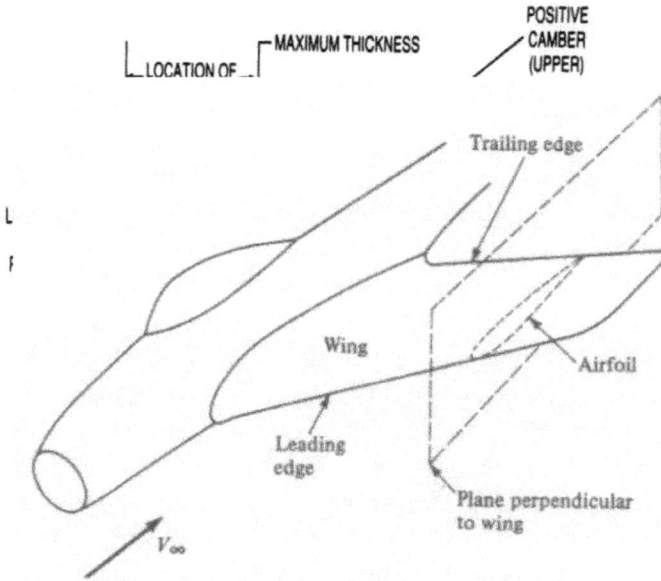

- The leading edge is the point at the front of the airfoil that has maximum curvature (minimum radius).
- The trailing edge is defined similarly as the point of maximum curvature at the rear of the airfoil.
- The chord line is the straight line connecting leading and trailing edges. The chord length, or simply chord, c, is the length of the chord line. That is the reference dimension of the airfoil section.
- The mean camber line or mean line is the locus of points midway between the upper and lower surfaces. Its shape depends on the thickness distribution along the chord.

NACA series
- Normally airfoils are classified by the National Advisory committee for aeronautics (NACA)
- NACA have been cataloged airfoils using 4 digit code Example NACA" WXYZ"

- W- maximum camber as % of chord length
- X- location of the maximum camber from the leading edge along the chord line
- Y & Z – maximum thickness in % of chord length
  Example -1   NACA 2412

Has a maximum mean camber of 2% of the chord at a position of four – tenths of the chord from leading edge with a maximum thickness of 12%of the chord.

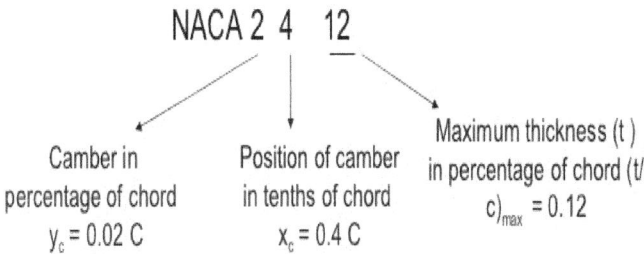

$$NACA\ 2\ 4\ \ \underline{12}$$

| Camber in percentage of chord $y_c = 0.02\ C$ | Position of camber in tenths of chord $x_c = 0.4\ C$ | Maximum thickness (t) in percentage of chord (t/c)$_{max}$ = 0.12 |

Aerodynamic forces

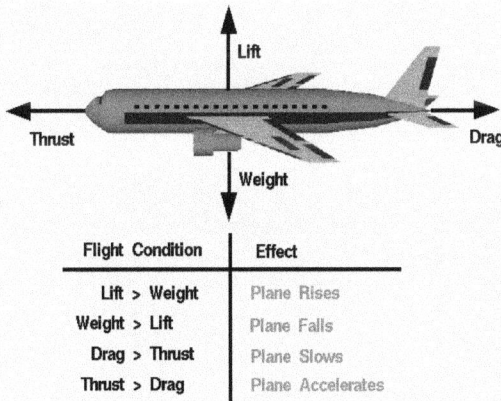

Flight Condition	Effect
Lift > Weight	Plane Rises
Weight > Lift	Plane Falls
Drag > Thrust	Plane Slows
Thrust > Drag	Plane Accelerates

Thrust—the forward force produced by the power plant/propeller or rotor. It opposes or overcomes the force of drag. As a general rule, it acts parallel to the longitudinal axis. However, this is not always the case, as explained later.

  Drag—a rearward, retarding force caused by disruption of airflow by the wing, rotor, fuselage, and other protruding objects. Drag opposes thrust and acts rearward parallel to the relative wind.

Weight—the combined load of the aircraft itself, the crew, the fuel, and the cargo or baggage. Weight pulls the aircraft downward because of the force of gravity. It opposes lift and acts vertically downward through the aircraft's center of gravity (CG).

Lift—opposes the downward force of weight, is produced by the dynamic effect of the air acting on the airfoil, and acts perpendicular to the flightpath through the center of lift.

LEADING AND TRAILING EDGE HIGH LIFTS DEVICES

- Trailing edge flap increase the camber by lowering the rear portion of the wing
- Slotted flap allows the air flow stick on the surface
- Eddies formed at the top surface may be eliminated using split flap like a lower jaw of mouth
- Many other type has invented which have its own advantages
- Few gave good increase in lift
- Few types gave good increase in lift to drag ratio

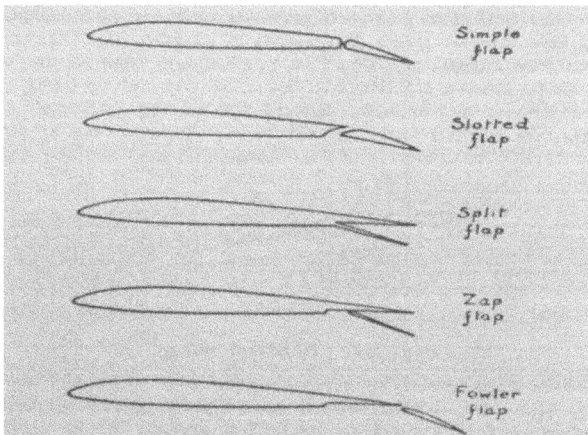

Slotted wing(slat)

- Stall is because of air flow breaking from the airfoil & forming eddies
- Slats are used to delay the stall of the wing
- Allowing air flow through the narrow gap(a venturi effect)

- The gap is slot and the small auxiliary aerofoil at the top surface is called slats

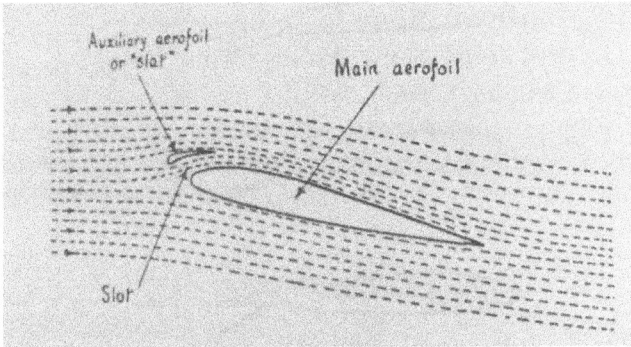

RELATION BETWEEN LIFT , DRAG AND ANGLE OF ATTACK CURVE

Drag:-

(a) Flap.

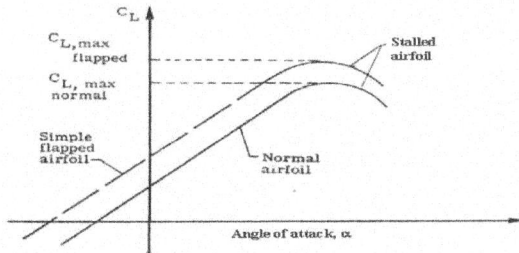

(b) Flap aerodynamic effects.

Drag is one of the four aerodynamic forces that act on a plane. For more information on aerodynamic forces click here. Drag is a restrictive force which opposes the motion of an aircraft. There are various types of drag depending upon their sources

Types of drag
- Parasite drag
- Form drag or pressure drag
- Skin friction drag

- Profile drag
- Interference drag
- Lift induced drag
- Wave drag

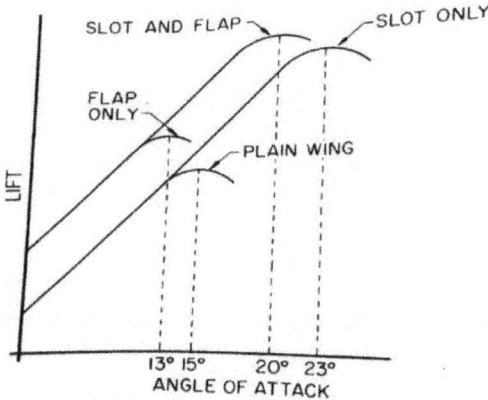

1. Parasite drag

Parasite drag is a drag produced due to the motion of an object through a fluid. With respect to aviation, the object is an aircraft and the fluid is the atmospheric air. Parasite drag occurs due to air molecules. Parasite drag is classified as form drag or pressure drag, skin friction drag and interference drag.

2. Form drag or pressure drag

Form drag is produced due to the shape of the object moving through the fluid. It depends on the cross section of an object. An object with a larger cross section and blunt shape will have a larger form drag whereas an object with a smaller cross section area and a sharper shape will have a lesser form drag.

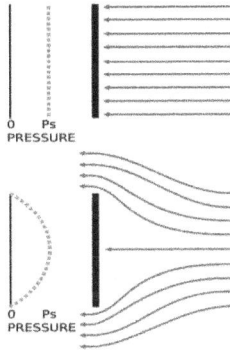

How is form drag reduced?

It can be reduced using smaller cross section area for making wings and by using aerodynamic shape for an aerofoil.

3. Skin friction drag

Skin friction drag is a drag produced due to friction between an object (aircraft) & fluid (atmospheric air). The rough surface will have high skin friction drag and conversely a smooth surface will have less skin friction drag.

How is skin friction drag reduced?

Making the aircraft skin smooth will reduce skin friction.

4. Profile drag

Profile drag is a sum of the form drag & skin friction drag.

5. Interference drag

Interference drag is produced due to the interference of two or more airflows having different speeds. And this drag is produced by the interference of different aircraft parts, that is, due to a mixture of airflow around wing and the airflow around the fuselage.

How interference drag is reduced?

This can be reduced by keeping the angle between these two below

90 degrees

6. Lift Induced drag

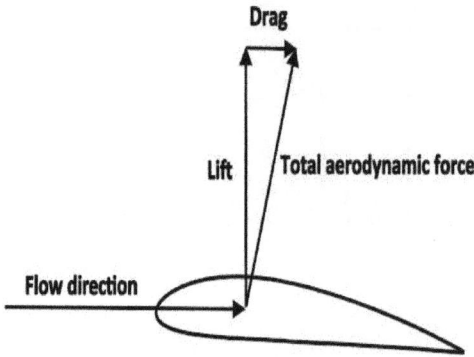

Lift induced drag

Lift is another aerodynamic force. It is a force which keeps an aircraft in the air and its magnitude is equal to the weight of the aircraft during stable flight. The direction of lift is perpendicular to the oncoming airflow towards the aircraft. Lift induced drag, as the name suggests, is a drag produced due to lift. At slower speed & higher angle of attack, aircraft will have more lift. But as the angle of attack increases, the air pushes the aircraft in the backward direction. This backward push is the induced drag. Technically speaking change in a vector direction of lift of the aircraft results in the formation of this type of drag.

Other types of induced drag are due to a mixture of airflow above and below the wing. The air flow mixes at the tips of the aircraft. We know that speed of airflow above the wing is higher than the speed of an airflow below the wing. Want to know the reason? Check here!

At the wing tips, these two air flows with variable speed, get mixed with each other which produces vortices at wing tips. The Reason for production of vortices is that high-pressure airflow gets pulled toward low-pressure airflow.

How is induced drag reduced?

Using winglet or shark-lets at wing tips.

8.Wave drag

Wave drag is generally produced at transonic speed (speed almost equals to speed of sound) & Supersonic speed (speed greater than speed of sound). Due to high speed of airflow, shock waves are produced. Shockwaves are nothing but the disturbance in the air. This disturbance increases drag of the aircraft known as wave drag.

How wave drag is reduced?

NASA F-15 -

Shock wave drag is one of the reason that at present time there are no supersonic passenger aircraft. Hence scientists are looking for the way to reduce shock wave drag. NASA is trying to reduce the shock wave drag by making aircraft noses sharp. NASA's quite spike F-15 is aircraft somewhat reduced the shockwave drag.

Drag Curve

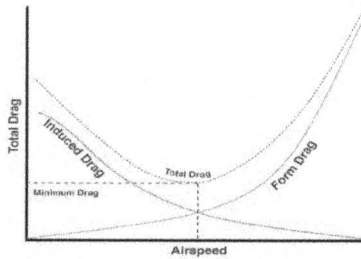

This drag curve shows the variation of different types of drag with respect to airspeed.

CL Vs. ALPHA CURVE : Symmetric airfoil

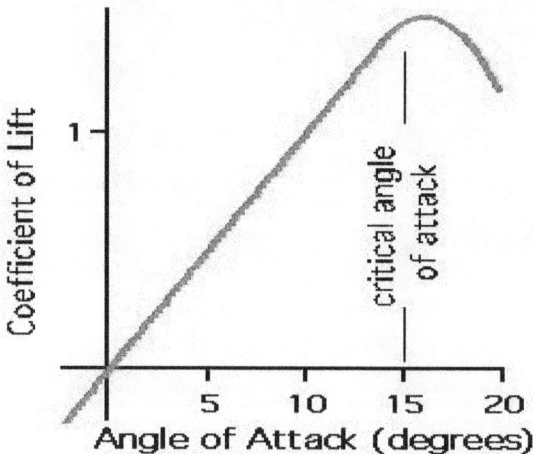

CL Vs. ALPHA CURVE : cambered airfoil

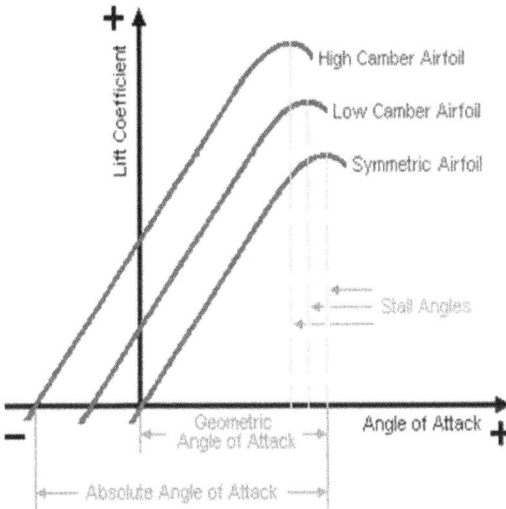

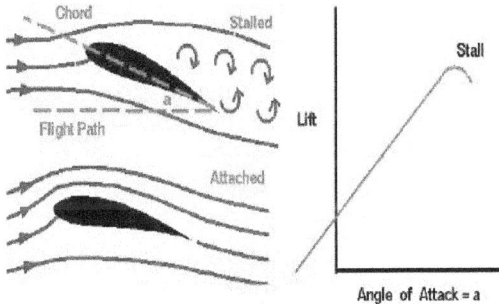

For small angles, lift is related to angle.
Greater Angle = Greater Lift

For larger angles, the lift relation is complex.
Included in Lift Coefficient

Range and Endurance and ceiling

Range

The maximum distance an aircraft can fly between takeoff and landing. As limited by fuel capacity in powered aircraft, or cross-country speed and environmental conditions in unpowered aircraft.

Endurance

The **flight endurance** record is the longest **amount of time** an aircraft of a particular category spent in **flight** without landing. It can be a solo event, or multiple people can take turns piloting the aircraft, as long as all pilots remain in the aircraft. In **aviation, endurance** is the maximum length of time that an **aircraft** can spend in cruising flight.

Ceiling
- The absolute ceiling is the altitude at which the (maximum) rate of climb goes to zero.
- The service ceiling is the altitude at which the maximum rate of climb is minimum 100 ft /min

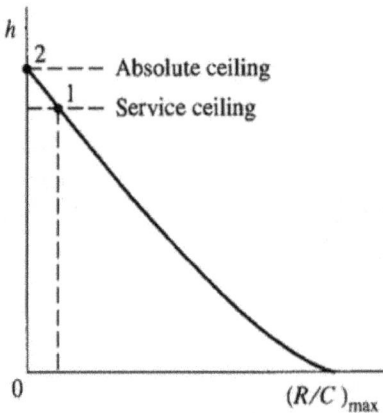

Sketch of variation of maximum rate of climb with altitude, illustrating absolute and service ceilings.

MANEUVERS - Aerobatics
- Aero plane should have the capable of Taxying , take off, climbing, level fly, turning, landing. **Aggressive aircraft** must be capable for more violent maneuvers which is called aerobatics. The readings recorded during aerobatics are used for theoretical calculation for further designs.
- *Loop*
    - swinging a bucket of water round in such a way water don't falls
    - Pilot like water.

- With out any danger of falling out

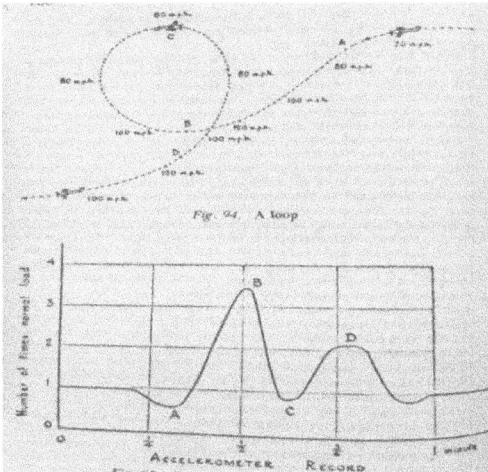

Fig. 94. A loop

- **Spin**
  - Olden days un solved problem ,
  - some of them not came out of spin what ever pilot do
  - Its an auto rotation , the vehicle is at or near to stalling angle
  - Wing loses lift & nose drops

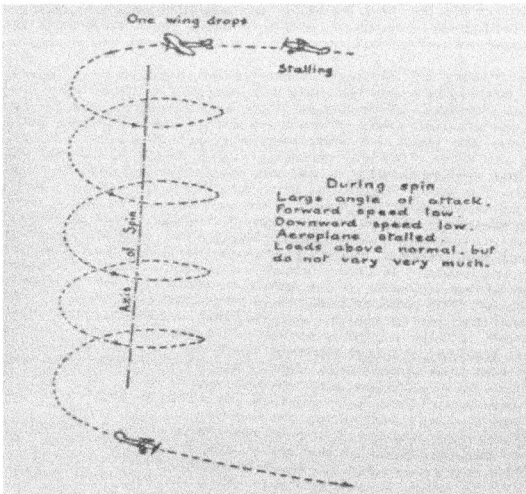

- **Roll**
  - Equally a spin but at horizontal axis
  - Fully controlled by the pilot (not accidently or auto)

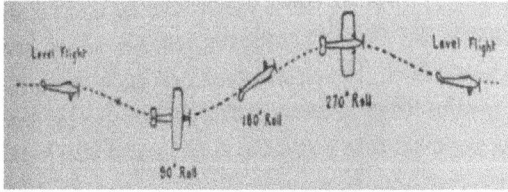

- *Inverted flight*
  - Normally maneuvered for the investigation of structural loading
  - As per airworthiness in aerobatic categories few aircraft should have the capability of inverted flight

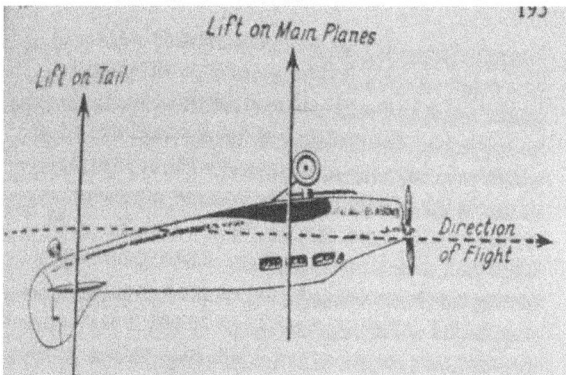

- *Nose dive*
  - Which feel much worse
  - True vertical dives are rarely performed in practice
  - Any dive at an angle greater than 70 degree to the horizontal seems near enough vertical to the pilot
  - Which is the greatest load encountered in the flight

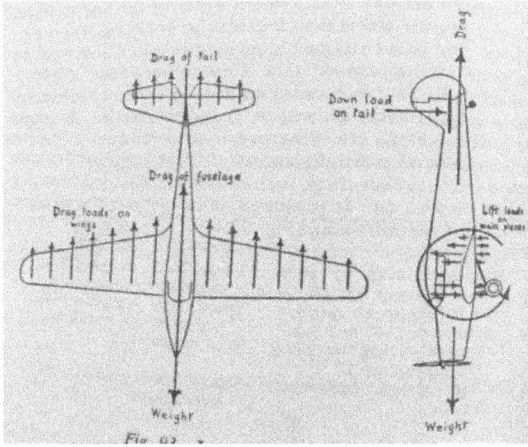

DIHEDRAL AND ANHEDRAL EFFECTS IN STABILITY

If the wing tips are higher than where the wings connect to the plane it is called a dihedral angle, most large airplanes are designed this way. This angle is used to increase roll stability. (This means that if the plane encounters a disturbance is can more easily return to its original position.) Anhedral angles are when the wing tips are lower than the wing base and are used on smaller planes like fighter planes. This angle increases the roll performance.

CHAPTER 3

AIRCRAFT CONSTRUCTION

Typical fuselage structure

The fuselage is the main structure, or body, of the aircraft. It provides space for personnel, cargo, controls, and most of the accessories. The power plant, wings, stabilizers, and landing gear are attached to it.

There are two general types of fuselage construction—welded steel truss and monocoque designs. The welded steel truss was used in smaller Navy aircraft, and it is still being used in some helicopters. The monocoque design relies largely on the strength of the skin, or covering, to carry various loads. The monocoque design may be divided into three classes—monocoque, semi-monocoque, and reinforced shell.

The true monocoque construction uses formers, frame assemblies, and bulkheads to give shape to the fuselage. However, the skin carries the primary stresses. Since no bracing members are present, the skin must be strong enough to keep the fuselage rigid. The biggest problem in monocoque construction is maintaining enough strength while keeping the weight within limits.

Semi-monocoque design overcomes the strength-to-weight problem of monocoque construction. In addition to having formers, frame assemblies, and bulkheads, the semi-monocoque construction has the skin reinforced by longitudinal members.

The reinforced shell has the skin reinforced by a complete framework of structural members. Different portions of the same fuselage may belong to any one of the three classes. Most are considered to be of semi-monocoque-type construction.

The semi-monocoque fuselage is constructed primarily of aluminum alloy, although steel and titanium are found in high-temperature areas. Primary bending loads are taken by the longerons, which usually extend across several points of support. The longerons are supplemented by other longitudinal members known as stringers. Stringers are more numerous and lightweight than longerons.

The vertical structural members are referred to as bulkheads, frames, and formers. The heavier vertical members are located at intervals to allow for concentrated loads. These members are also found at points where fittings are used to attach other units, such as the wings and stabilizers.

The stringers are smaller and lighter than longerons and serve as fill-ins. They have some rigidity but are chiefly used for giving shape and for attachment of skin. The strong, heavy longerons hold the bulkheads and formers. The bulkheads and formers hold the stringers. All of these join together to form a rigid fuselage framework. Stringers and longerons prevent tension and compression stresses from bending the fuselage.

The skin is attached to the longerons, bulkheads, and other structural members and carries part of the load. The fuselage skin thickness varies with the load carried and the stresses sustained at particular location.

There are a number of advantages in using the semi-monocoque fuselage. The bulkhead, frames, stringers, and longerons aid in the design and construction of a streamlined fuselage. They add to the strength and rigidity of the structure. The main advantage of the

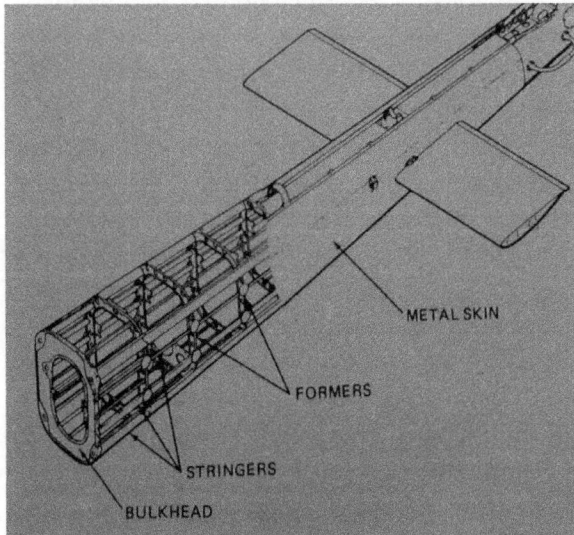

semi-monocoque construction is that it depends on many structural members for strength and rigidity. Because of its stressed skin construction, a semi-monocoque fuselage can withstand damage and still be strong enough to hold together.

Basic terminologies

- Bulkhead : A heavy structural member in the fuselage to contain pressure or fluids or to disperse concentrated loads. A heavy circumferential frame, which may or may not be entirely closed by a web.

- Longeron : A principal longitudinal member of the framing of an a/c fuselage or nacelle. It is as usually continuous across a number of points of support.

- Strut : A supporting brace that bears compression loads, or both , as in a fuselage between the longerons or in a landing gear to transmit the airplane loads.

- Rib: A fore and aft member of an airfoil structure(wing or aileron) of an a/c used to give the airfoil section its form and to transmit the load from the skin to the spars.

- Spar: A principal span wise beam in the structure of a wing, stabilizer, rudder, or elevator. It is usually the primary load-carrying member in the structure.

- Stringer : Longitudinal member in the fuselage or span wise members in the wing to transmit skin loads into the body frames or wing ribs.

Wing configuration

Wings develop the major portion of the lift of a heavier-than-air aircraft. Wing structures carry some of the heavier loads found in the aircraft structure. The particular design of a wing depends on many factors, such as the size, weight, speed, rate of climb, and use of the aircraft. The wing must be constructed so that it holds its aerodynamics shape under the extreme stresses of combat maneuvers or wing loading.

Wing construction is similar in most modern aircraft. In its simplest form, the wing is a frame work made up of spars and ribs and covered with metal. Spars are the main structural members of the wing.

They extend from the fuselage to the tip of the wing. All the load carried by the wing is taken up by the spars. The spars are designed to have great bending strength. Ribs give the wing section its shape, and they transmit the air load from the wing covering to the spars. Ribs extend from the leading edge to the trailing edge of the wing. In addition to the main spars, some wings have a false spar to support the ailerons and flaps. Most aircraft wings have a removable tip, which streamlines the outer end of the wing.

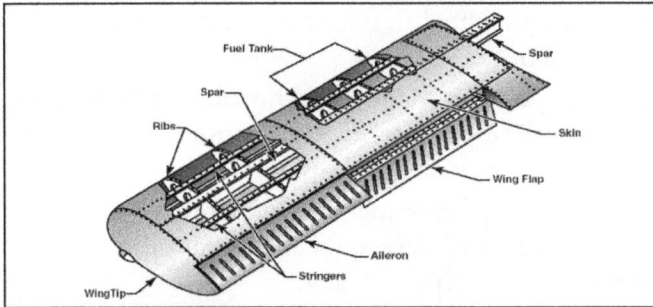

Wing position

- Low wing : located on the base of the fuselage - allows good visibility up wards – give tendency to float further before landing (good CG)
- Mid wing : its is located at the mid way up the fuselage – is aerodynamically most balanced position - but it may affect the useful fuselage volume
- High wing : wing upper surface will be on or above the fuselage (cargo-planes)
- Shoulder wing : located between high and mid wing but not on the very top of the fuselage

High-wing

Mid-wing

Low-wing

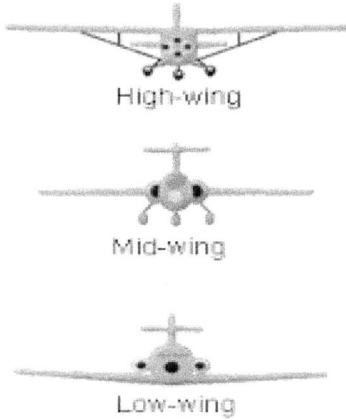

Landing gear configurations

The landing gear system consists of three retractable landing gear assemblies. Each main landing gear has a conventional air-oil shock strut, a wheel brake assembly, and a wheel and tire assembly. The nose landing gear has a conventional air-oil shock strut, a shimmy damper, and a wheel and tire assembly. The shock strut is designed to absorb the shock that would otherwise be transmitted to the airframe during landing, taxiing, and takeoff. The air-oil strut is used on all naval aircraft. This type of strut has two telescoping cylinders filled with hydraulic fluid and compressed air or nitrogen. The main landing gear is equipped with brakes for stopping the aircraft and assisting the pilot in steering the aircraft on the ground. The nose gear of most aircraft can be steered from the cockpit. This provides greater ease and safety on the runway when landing and taking off and on the taxi way in taxiing.

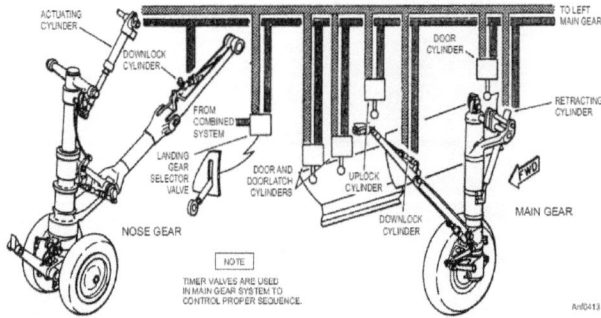

Metallic and non-metallic materials
METALLIC MATERIALS
The most common metals used in aircraft construction are aluminum, magnesium, titanium, steel, and their alloys.

Alloys
An alloy is composed of two or more metals. The metal present in the alloy in the largest amount is called the *base metal*. All other metals added to the base metal are called *alloying elements*. Adding the alloying elements may result in a change in the properties of the base metal. For example, pure aluminum is relatively soft and weak. However, adding small amounts or copper, manganese, and magnesium will increase aluminum's strength many times. Heat treatment can increase or decrease an alloy's strength and hardness. Alloys are important to the aircraft industry. They provide materials with properties that pure metals do not possess.

Aluminum
Aluminum alloys are widely used in modern aircraft construction. Aluminum alloys are valuable because they have a high strength-to-weight ratio. Aluminum alloys are corrosion resistant and comparatively easy to fabricate. The outstanding characteristic of aluminum is its lightweight.

Magnesium
Magnesium is the world's lightest structural metal. It is a silvery-white material that weighs two-thirds as much as aluminum. Magnesium is used to make helicopters. Magnesium's low resistance to corrosion has limited its use in conventional aircraft.

Titanium

Titanium is a lightweight, strong, corrosion resistant metal. Recent developments make titanium ideal for applications where aluminum alloys are too weak and stainless steel is too heavy. Additionally , titanium is unaffected by long exposure to seawater and marine atmosphere.

Steel Alloys

Alloy steels used in aircraft construction have great strength, more so than other fields of engineering would require. These materials must withstand the forces that occur on today's modern aircraft. These steels contain small percentages of carbon, nickel, chromium, vanadium, and molybdenum. High-tensile steels will stand stress of 50 to 150 tons per square inch without failing. Such steels are made into tubes, rods, and wires. Another type of steel used extensively is stainless steel. Stainless steel resists corrosion and is particularly valuable for use in or near water.

NONMETALLIC MATERIALS

In addition to metals, various types of plastic materials are found in aircraft construction. Some of these plastics include transparent plastic, reinforced plastic, composite, and carbon-fiber materials.

Transparent Plastic

Transparent plastic is used in canopies, windshields, and other transparent enclosure. At approximately 225°F, transparent plastic becomes soft and pliable.

Reinforced Plastic

Reinforced plastic is used in the construction of radomes, wingtips, stabilizer tips, antenna covers, and flight controls. Reinforced plastic has a high strength-to-weight ratio and is resistant to mildew and rot. Because it is easy to fabricate, it is equally suitable for other parts of the aircraft.

Reinforced plastic is a sandwich-type material. It is made up of two outer facings and a center
layer. The facings are made up of several layers of glass cloth, bonded together with a liquid resin. The core material (center layer)

consists of a honeycomb structure made of glass cloth. Reinforced plastic is fabricated into a variety of cell sizes.

Composite and Carbon Fiber Materials

High-performance aircraft require an extra high strength-to-weight ratio material. Fabrication of composite materials satisfies this special requirement. Composite materials are constructed by using several layers of bonding materials (graphite epoxy or boron epoxy). These materials are mechanically fastened to conventional substructures. Another type of composite construction consists of thin graphite epoxy skins bonded to an aluminum honeycomb core. Carbon fiber is extremely strong, thin fiber made by heating synthetic fibers, such as rayon, until charred, and then layering in cross sections.

CHAPTER 4

FLIGHT VEHICLE COMPONENTS AND SYSTEM

Components of an airplane and their function, control surface and basic instruments for flying, Conventional control system, types of control surface actuation system, Basic of hydraulics and pneumatics systems, fly by wire, fly by light and acoustic concept, Aircraft pressurization

COMPONENTS OF AN AIRPLANE AND THEIR FUNCTION

- Aileron: To roll left & right.
- Aileron Trim: To roll left & right a little.
- Anti-Collision Warning Beacon: A red light to warn other aircraft and help prevent mid-air collisions.
- A.P.U. Exhaust: This is the exhaust pipe for the A.P.U. (Auxiliary Power Unit). The A.P.U. is an engine in the tail of the aircraft. It is used only on the ground. It generates electrical power for the aircraft and is used to start the jet engines.
- Cockpit / Flight Deck: In this room, pilots aviate, communicate, and navigate.
- Elevator Trim: To pitch up & down a little.
- Engine Cowling: The main cover or housing of the engine.
- Engine Mounting: Used to fix the engine to the wing.
- Flap: To increase lift during take-off and landing. Pilots extend the flaps to increase the wing's area. This increases the lift.
- Fuselage: The body or structure of the aircraft.

- Horizontal Stabiliser: Stabilises the aircraft around the lateral axis.
- Landing Gear: Pilots extend or retract the landing gear (wheels) during take-off and landing.
- Leading Edge: Front section of the wing.
- Main Elevator: To pitch up & down.
- Main Rudder: To yaw (turn) left & right.
- Nose Gear: The front wheels of the aircraft. Aircraft also have MAIN GEAR (wheels under the aircraft's wings) and sometimes BODY GEAR (wheels under the aircraft's body).
- Propeller: Gives an aircraft thrust or power.
- Pylons: Used to stabilise the air flow behind the wing. Without pylons, the air is unstable. This makes drag, and reduces the aircraft's speed and performance.
- Radome: The aircraft's radar is inside the radome or nose of the aircraft.
- Rudder Trim: To yaw left & right a little.
- Speed Brakes / Air Brakes: Used to slow the plane in the air and while landing.
- Spoilers: Used to destroy lift and keep the plane on the ground. This is important while landing. Without spoilers, the plane bounces on the runway. This can damage the landing gear. Some pilots prefer hard landings to help prevent bounce.
- Stabiliser Trim: To increase the angle of attack (A.O.A.). Basically, the angle of attack is the angle the wing hits the air.
- Trailing Edge: Back section of the wing.
- Vertical Stabiliser: Stabilises the aircraft around the vertical axis.
- Vortex Generator: Used to create lift in areas of the wing that have no or very little lift, for example, next to the engine mounting.
- Winglet: Used to reduce the vortex at the end of the wing. A vortex is unstable circular air. It makes drag, and reduces the aircraft's speed and performance.
- Wing Tip: The end or tip of the wing.

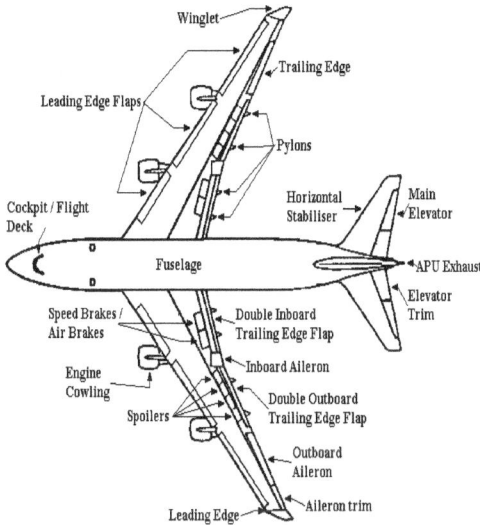

CONTROL SURFACE

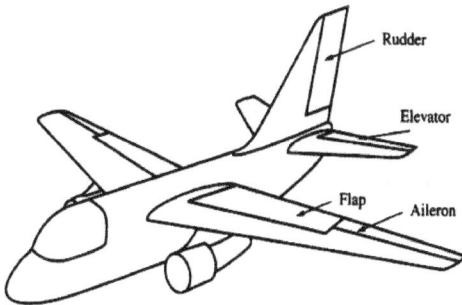

Ailerons

Ailerons are mounted on the trailing edge of each wing near the wingtips and move in opposite directions. When the pilot moves the stick left, or turns the wheel counter-clockwise, the left aileron goes up and the right aileron goes down. A raised aileron reduces lift on that wing and a lowered one increases lift, so moving the stick left causes the left wing to drop and the right wing to rise. This causes the aircraft to roll to the left and begin to turn to the left. Centering the stick returns the ailerons to neutral maintaining the bank angle. The aircraft will continue to turn until opposite aileron motion returns the bank angle to zero to fly straight.

The ailerons primarily control roll. Whenever lift is increased, induced drag is also increased. When the stick is moved left to roll the aircraft to the left, the right aileron is lowered which increases lift on the right wing and therefore increases induced drag on the right wing. Using ailerons causes adverse yaw, meaning the nose of the aircraft yaws in a direction opposite to the aileron application. When moving the stick to the left to bank the wings, adverse yaw moves the nose of the aircraft to the right. Adverse yaw is more pronounced for light aircraft with long wings, such as gliders. It is counteracted by the pilot with the rudder. Differential ailerons are ailerons which have been rigged such that the down going aileron deflects less than the upward-moving one, reducing adverse yaw.

Elevator

The elevator is a moveable part of the horizontal stabilizer, hinged to the back of the fixed part of the horizontal tail. The elevators move up and down together. When the pilot pulls the stick backward, the elevators go up. Pushing the stick forward causes the elevators to go down. Raised elevators push down on the tail and cause the nose to pitch up. This makes the wings fly at a higher angle of attack, which generates more lift and more drag. Centering the stick returns the elevators to neutral and stops the change of pitch.

Rudder

The rudder is typically mounted on the trailing edge of the vertical stabilizer, part of the empennage. When the pilot pushes the left pedal, the rudder deflects left. Pushing the right pedal causes the rudder to deflect right. Deflecting the rudder right pushes the tail left and causes the nose to yaw to the right. Centering the rudder pedals returns the rudder to neutral and stops the yaw.

If rudder is continuously applied in level flight the aircraft will yaw initially in the direction of the applied rudder – the primary effect of rudder. After a few seconds the aircraft will tend to bank in the direction of yaw.

This arises initially from the increased speed of the wing opposite to the direction of yaw and the reduced speed of the other wing. The faster wing generates more lift and so rises, while the other wing tends to go down because of generating less lift. Continued application of rudder sustains rolling tendency because the aircraft flying at an angle to the airflow - skidding towards the forward wing. When applying right rudder in an aircraft with dihedral the left hand wing will have increased angle of attack and the right hand wing will have decreased angle of attack which will result in a roll to the right. An aircraft with anhedral will show the opposite effect. This effect of the rudder is commonly used in model aircraft where if sufficient dihedral or polyhedral is included in the wing design, primary roll control such as ailerons may be omitted altogether.

BASIC INSTRUMENTS FOR FLYING

The flight instruments are the instruments in the cockpit of an aircraft that provide the pilot with flight parameters. The flight instruments are used in conditions of poor visibility when the pilot loses visual reference outside the aircraft.

1. Airspeed indicator

2. Attitude indicator

3. Altimeter

4. Turn coordinator

5. Heading indicator

6. Vertical speed indicator

1. Airspeed indicator

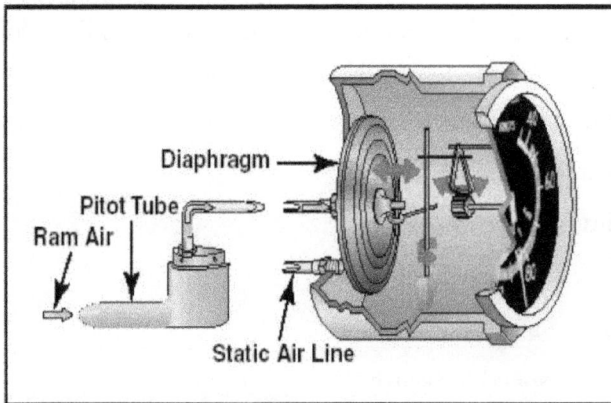

The airspeed indicator (ASI) displays the speed at which the airplane is moving through the air. The direct instrument reading obtained from the airspeed indicator, uncorrected for variations in atmospheric density, installation error, or instrument error. Manufacturers use this airspeed as the basis for determining airplane performance. The airspeed indicator is a sensitive differential pressure gauge which measures and shows the difference between impact pressure from Pitot tube, and static pressure from static line (the undisturbed atmospheric pressure at current flight level).

These two pressures will be equal when the airplane is parked on the ground in calm air. When the airplane moves through the air, the pressure on the pitot line becomes greater than the pressure in the static lines. This difference in pressure is registered by the airspeed pointer on the face of the instrument, which is calibrated in miles per hour, knots, or both.

The airspeed indicator can display also other speed information:

- White arc: This arc is commonly referred to as the flap operating range since its lower limit represents the full flap stall speed and its upper limit provides the maximum flap speed (Approaches and landings are usually flown at speeds within the white arc.
- Lower limit of white arc (VS0): The stalling speed or the minimum steady flight speed in the landing configuration. In small airplanes, this is the power-off stall speed at the maximum landing weight in the landing configuration (gear and flaps down).
- Upper limit of the white arc (VFE): The maximum speed with the flaps extended.
- Green arc: This is the normal operating range of the airplane. Most flying occurs within this range.
- Lower limit of green arc (VS1): The stalling speed or the minimum steady flight speed obtained in a specified configuration. For most airplanes, this is the power-off stall speed at the maximum takeoff weight in the clean configuration (gear up, if retractable, and flaps up).
- Upper limit of green arc (VNO): The maximum structural cruising speed. Do not exceed this speed except in smooth air.
- Yellow arc: Caution range. Fly within this range only in smooth air, and then, only with caution.
- Red line (VNE): Never exceed speed. Operating above this speed is prohibited since it may result in damage or structural failure.

2. Attitude indicator

The attitude indicator displays a picture of the attitude of the aircraft. There is also a miniature aircraft (orange line) and horizon bar representation.

The horizon is displayed using a white line which separates the instrument in two parts:

- the blue one which represents the sky
- the brown one which represents the earth.

The relationship of the miniature aircraft to the horizon bar is the same as the relationship of the real aircraft to the actual horizon. The instrument gives an instantaneous indication of even the smallest changes in attitude.

The gyro in the attitude indicator is mounted in a horizontal plane and depends upon rigidity in space for its operation. The horizon bar represents the true horizon. This bar is fixed to the gyro and remains in a horizontal plane as the aircraft is pitched or banked about its lateral or longitudinal axis, indicating the attitude of the aircraft relative to the true horizon.

3. Altimeter

The altimeter displays the altitude of the airplane above mean sea level (MSL) when properly adjusted to the current pressure setting. The value is expressed in feet (ft); it can be meter (m) in some aircraft. In aircraft, an aneroid barometer measures the atmospheric pressure from a static port outside the aircraft. Air pressure decreases with an increase of altitude—approximately 100 hectopascals per 800 meters or one inch of mercury per 1000 feet near sea level.

The analogic altimeter has 2 needles:

- The longest one for the hundreds of feet
- The shortest one for the thousands of feet

4. Turn coordinator

The turn coordinator (turn and balance indicator) are essentially two aircraft flight instruments in one device. They each act as a rate of turn indicator that displays the rate the aircraft heading is changing and a balance indicator or slip indicator that displays the slip or skid of the turn.

The turn indicator display contains hash marks where the needle may align during a turn. When the needle is lined up with these hash marks, the aircraft is performing a standard rate turn.

The standard rate (or named rate "one") for most airplanes is three degrees per second or two minutes per 360 degrees of turn (a complete circle). This is marked as "2 min" on the display.

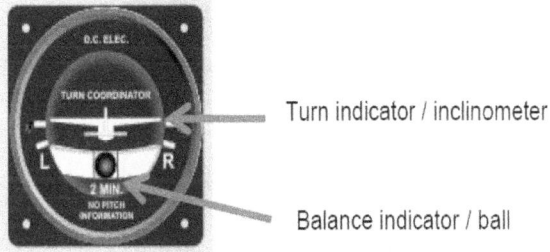

Turn indicator / inclinometer

Balance indicator / ball

The balance indicator information of the aircraft is often obtained by an inclinometer, which is recognized as the ball in a tube

| Standard left turn | No turn in progress | Standard right turn |

In a standard turn, the ball in the balance indicator is always cantered.

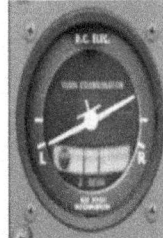

| Aircraft skidding to inside of turn | Coordinated Turn | Aircraft slipping to outside of turn |

The turn coordinator should be used as a performance instrument when the attitude indicator has failed.

5. Heading indicator

The heading indicator is used to inform the pilot of the aircraft's heading.

It is sometimes referred to by its older names, the directional gyro and also direction indicator.

The heading indicator is fundamentally a mechanical instrument designed to facilitate the use of the magnetic compass. Errors in the magnetic compass are numerous, making straight flight and precision turns to headings difficult to accomplish, particularly in turbulent air.

To remedy errors in the magnetic compass reading, the pilot will typically manoeuvre the airplane with reference to the heading indicator, as the gyroscopic heading indicator is unaffected by dip and acceleration errors.

The primary means of establishing the heading in most small aircraft is the magnetic compass, which, however, suffers from several types of errors, including that created by the "dip" or downward slope of the Earth's magnetic field. Dip whenever the aircraft is in a bank, or during acceleration, making it difficult to use in any flight condition other than perfectly straight and level.

The pilot will periodically reset the heading indicator to the heading shown on the magnetic compass.

6. Vertical speed indicator

The vertical speed indicator (VSI), called also variometer or a vertical velocity indicator, indicates whether the airplane is climbing, descending, or in level flight. The rate of climb or descent is indicated in feet per minute. If properly calibrated, the VSI indicates zero in level flight.

The VSI does not display immediately an accurate indication of a climbing or descending rate. There exists a lag or a time between the initial changes in the rate of climb/descent and the display of this new rate.

CONVENTIONAL CONTROL SYSTEM

- Pneumatic actuator
- Electrical system
- Hydraulic actuator
- Mechanical system without feedback
- Fly by wire system

HYDRAULIC ACTUATORS

Hydraulic actuators or hydraulic cylinders typically involve a hollow cylinder having a piston inserted in it. The two sides of the piston are alternately pressurized/de-pressurized to achieve controlled precise linear displacement of the piston and in turn the entity connected to the piston. The physical linear displacement is only along the axis of piston/cylinder. This design is based on the principles of hydraulics. A familiar example of a manually operated hydraulic actuator is a hydraulic car jack. Typically though, the term "hydraulic actuator" refers to a device controlled by a hydraulic pump. The disadvantage of these actuators is that it requires separate oil chamber in order to perform actuation. It can leak and also requires position feedback for repeatability.

A – Aileron   B – Pilot Stick
C – Elevator   D – Rudder

PNEUMATIC ACTUATORS

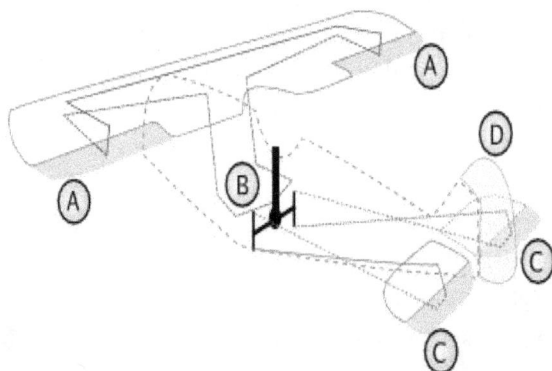

A pneumatic actuator converts energy (in the for m of compressed air, typically) into motion. The motion can be rotary or linear, depending on the type of actuator. A Pneumatic actuator mainly consists of a piston, a cylinder, and valves or ports. The piston is covered by a diaphragm, or seal, which keeps the air in the upper portion of the cylinder , allowing air pressure to force the diaphragm downward, moving the piston underneath, which in turn moves the valve stem, which is linked to the internal parts of the actuator. Pneumatic actuators may only have one spot for a signal input, top or bottom, depending on action required. The force required by the stem is large and hence it may make the stem system to fail. It also requires a separate air chamber.

DIGITAL FLIGHT CONTROL SYSTEM

The digital flight control system is designed using electronic actuators with feedback system and digital micro controllers. The digital flight control systems are implemented using digital technology, the pilot input signals being transmitted as serial digital data using avionics data bus networks. The signals   data   are   subsequently   processed   by   digital microcontroller s in the flight control computers. A microcontroller is a computer-on-a-chip, or a single-chip computer. Micro suggests that the device is small, and controller tells that the device might be used to control objects, processes, or events. Another term to describe a microcontroller is embedded controller, because the microcontroller and its support circuits are often built into, or embedded in, the devices they control. Microcontrollers are found in many common application areas, including domestic appliances such as microwaves, televisions and television remote control units, stereo units, and increasingly in automobiles for engine control, passenger heater unit control, display instrumentation and many other tasks. The widespread availability of microcontrollers is a testament to their flexibility and low unit cost.

Systematic block diagram for maneuvering aircraft using digital flight control system

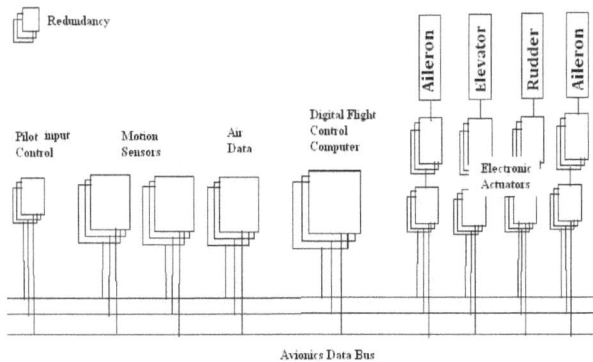

Avionics Data Bus

ADVANTAGE OF DIGITAL FLIGHT CONTROL SYSTEM

The advantage of Digital flight control systems over the Mechanical Systems are Easy to Installation and maintenance Digital systems do not have the problem of friction Digital systems are not affected by bending or vibration of aircraft.

• Weight Reductions

- Hardware economy
- Flexibility
- Digital Avionics data buses

FLY BY LIGHT SYSTEM

With the intensity of the light reflected , control surface actuation can be done more effectively. Moreover the usage of wires can be eliminated

Systematic block diagram for maneuvering aircraft using light intensity

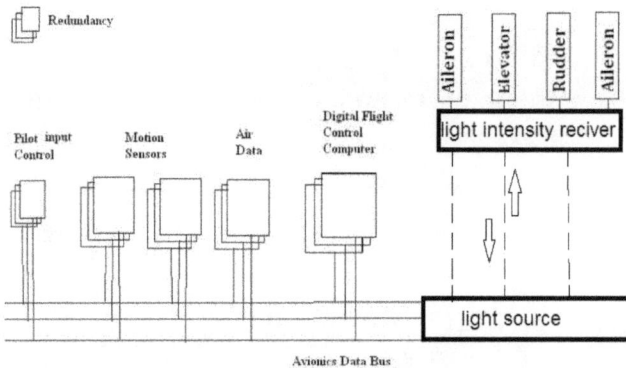

ADVANTAGE OF FLY BY LIGHT FLIGHT CONTROL SYSTEM

The advantage of fly by light flight control systems over the digital Systems are…..

- Easy to Installation and maintenance
- Light systems do not have the problem of friction
- Light systems are not affected by bending or vibration of aircraft.
- Weight Reductions
- Hardware economy
- Flexibility

- Reliable
- Quick and Accurate

FLY BY ACOUSTICS

With the intensity of the sound reflected , control surface actuation can be done more effectively. Moreover the usage of wires can be eliminated.

Systematic block diagram for maneuvering aircraft using sound source

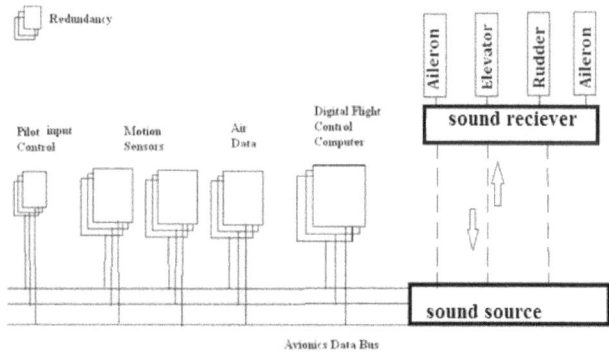

AIRCRAFT PRESSURIZATION

- Pressurize means to increase the pressure.
- Pressurization is the act of increasing the air pressure inside a space
  (example: an aircraft cabin)
- The cabin pressurization system in today's aircraft is designed to provide a safe and comfortable cabin environment at cruising altitudes that can reach up to 40,000 feet.
- Also this system is important to protect crews & passengers from the physiological risks of high altitudes such as hypoxia, decompression sickness & trapped gas.
- At higher altitude, the outside atmospheric pressure is very low, thus give difficulties to our body system to function normally.

Aircraft cabin pressurization can be controlled via two different modes of operation. The first is the isobaric mode, which works to maintain cabin altitude at a single pressure despite the changing altitude of the aircraft. For example, the flight crew may select to maintain a cabin altitude of 8,000 feet (10.92 psi). In the isobaric mode, the cabin pressure is established at the 8,000 foot level and remains at this level.

The second mode of pressurization control is the constant differential mode, which controls cabin pressure to maintain a constant pressure difference between the air pressure inside the cabin and the ambient air pressure, regardless of aircraft altitude changes. The constant differential mode pressure differential is lower than the maximum differential pressure for which the airframe is designed, keeping the integrity of the pressure vessel intact.

When in isobaric mode, the pressurization system maintains the cabin altitude selected by the crew. This is the condition for normal operations. But when the aircraft climbs beyond a certain altitude, maintaining the selected cabin altitude may result in a differential pressure above that for which the airframe was designed. In this case, the mode of pressurization automatically switches from isobaric to constant differential mode. This occurs before the cabin's max differential pressure limit is reached. A constant differential pressure is then maintained, regardless of the selected cabin altitude.

Cabin Pressure Controller

The cabin pressure controller is the device used to control the cabin air pressure. Older aircraft use strictly pneumatic means for controlling cabin pressure. Selections for the desired cabin altitude, rate of cabin altitude change, and barometric pressure setting are all made directly to the pressure controller from pressurization panel in the cockpit.

CHAPTER 5

AVIATION POWER PLANT

ENGINES

The two most common types of engines used in aircrafts are the reciprocating engine and the turbine engine. Reciprocating engines, also called piston engines, are generally used in smaller helicopters. Most training helicopters use reciprocating engines because they are relatively simple and inexpensive to operate. Turbine engines are more powerful and are used in a wide variety of helicopters. They produce a tremendous amount of power for their size but are generally more expensive to operate.

RECIPROCATING ENGINE

The reciprocating engine consists of a series of pistons connected to a rotating crank shaft. As the pistons move up and down, the crankshaft rotates. The reciprocating engine gets its name from the back-and-forth movement of its internal parts. The four-stroke engine is the most common type, and refers to the four different cycles the engine undergoes to produce power. When the piston moves away from the cylinder head on the intake stroke, the intake valve opens and a mixture of fuel and air is drawn into the combustion chamber. As the cylinder moves back towards the cylinder head, the in take valve closes, and the fuel/air mixture is com- pressed. When compression is nearly complete, the spark plugs fire and the compressed mixture is ignited to begin the power stroke. The rapidly expanding gases from the controlled burning of the fuel/air mixture drive the piston away from the cylinder head, thus pro- viding power to rotate the crankshaft. The piston then moves back toward the cylinder head on the exhaust stroke where the burned gasses are expelled through the opened exhaust valve.

Even when the engine is operate data fairly low speed, the four-stroke cycle takes place several hundred times each minute. In a four-cylinder engine, each cylinder operates on a different stroke. Continuous rotation of a crankshaft is maintained by the precise timing of the power strokes in each cylinder.

Types of power plants

- CI – Combustion ignition engine

- diesel engine
- SI- Spark ignition engine
- Petrol engines
- IC- internal combustion engines
- Piston engines , jet engines
- EC- external combustion engine
- steam **engine**

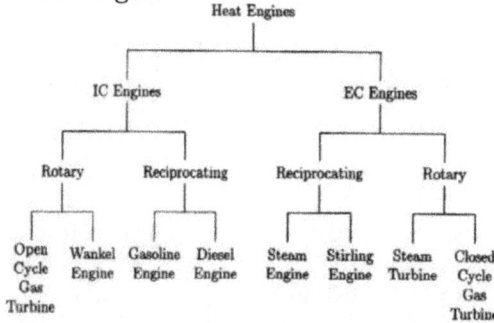

Heat Engines

IC Engines — EC Engines

Rotary — Reciprocating — Reciprocating — Rotary

Open Cycle Gas Turbine | Wankel Engine | Gasoline Engine | Diesel Engine | Steam Engine | Stirling Engine | Steam Turbine | Closed Cycle Gas Turbine

SI Engines
- SI engines draw fuel and air into the cylinder.
- Air intake is throttled to the SI engine
- Upper compression ratio in SI engines is limited by the auto ignition temperature
- Flame front in SI engines smooth and controlled.

CI Engines
- Fuel must be injected into the cylinder at the desired time of combustion in CI engines.
- no throttling in CI engines.
- Compression ratios must be high enough to cause auto-ignition
- compressed to pressure about 4 Mpa and temperature about 800 K.
- CI combustion is quick and uncontrolled at the beginning
- The valve timing in both CI and SI are similar.
- Diesel-cycle and four-stroke gasoline engines
- Share the same basic principles
- Gasoline engine: spark ignition (S.I.) engine
- Diesel, compression ignition engines: do not use a spark to ignite fuel
- Diesel engines
- Compression ratio: comparison between volume of cylinder and combustion chamber
- Can run at very lean air-fuel mixtures at idle
- Have high particulate emissions
- Basic components of piston engine :
- Cylinder head

- Cylinder
- Piston
- Piston rings
- Crank shaft
- Cam shaft
- Valve

Factor	SI Engine	CI Engine
Intake/compression	Air and fuel	Air only
Speed control	Throttled air-fuel mixture	Air unthrottled, fuel control only
Mixture uniformity	Nearly homogeneous	Very heterogeneous
Equivalence ratio	0.85 to 1.25	0 to 0.7
Exhaust temperature	Higher	Lower
Compression ratio range	7 to 10	14 to 20
Required strength	Lower	Higher
Relative efficiency at full load	1.0	1.4
Relative $P_b / (D_e N_e)$	1.0	$0.7 \times 1.4 = 0.98$

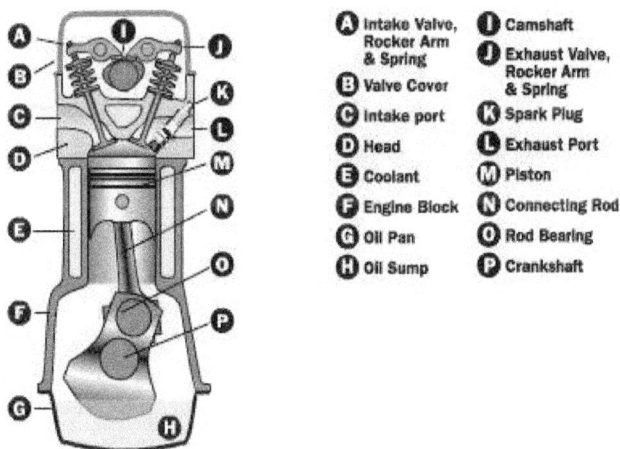

A Intake Valve, Rocker Arm & Spring
B Valve Cover
C Intake port
D Head
E Coolant
F Engine Block
G Oil Pan
H Oil Sump
I Camshaft
J Exhaust Valve, Rocker Arm & Spring
K Spark Plug
L Exhaust Port
M Piston
N Connecting Rod
O Rod Bearing
P Crankshaft

©2000 How Stuff Works, Inc.

Cylinder block

- Cylinder is the main body of IC engine.
- Cylinder is a part in which the intake of fuel, compression and burning take place
- Guide the piston

Cylinder head

- The top end of cylinder is closed by means of removable cylinder head
- Valves holes will be located
- Inlet exhaust ports

Piston

- A piston is fitted to each cylinder
- Face to receive gas pressure / temperature
- Transmit the thrust to the connecting rod.
- It is the prime mover in the engine

Piston rings

- A piston must be a fairly loose fit in the cylinder so it can move freely inside the cylinder.
- To provide a good sealing fit and less friction resistance between the piston and cylinder,
- pistons are equipped with piston rings.
- These rings are fitted in grooves which have been cut in the piston

Connecting rod

- Connecting rod connects the piston to crankshaft
- It converts the reciprocating motion of the piston into rotary motion of crankshaft.
- Big end is connected to the crankshaft
- the small end is connected to the piston by use of piston pin.

Crankshaft

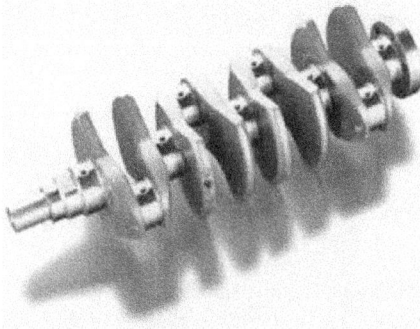

- The crankshaft of an internal combustion engine receives the efforts or thrust supplied by
- piston to the connecting rod and converts the reciprocating motion of piston into rotary
- motion of crankshaft. The crankshaft mounts in bearing so it can rotate freely.

Crankcase

- contains the crankshaft and crankshaft bearing is called crankcase.
- It serves as the part lubricating system.
- it is called as oil sump

Valves

All Types of Valves

- To control the inlet and exhaust of internal combustion engine,
- The number of valves depends on the number of cylinders.
- Two valves are used for each cylinder one for inlet of air-fuel mixture inside the cylinder and other for exhaust of combustion gases.
- The valves are fitted in the port at the cylinder head by use of strong spring.
- This spring keep them closed. Both valves usually open inwards.

Piston Engine Classifications

- Piston engines all have the same basic parts
- Differences in design
- Engine classifications
- Cylinder arrangement
- Cooling system
- Valve location and cam location
- Combustion
- Power type
- Ignition system
- Number of strokes per cycle

Cylinder Arrangement

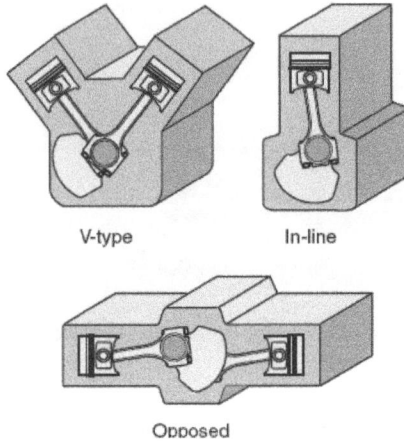

V-type   In-line

Opposed

- Automobile engines
- Have three or more cylinders
- Cylinders are arranged in several ways
- In-line: all cylinders arranged in one row
- "V" arrangement: cylinders are cast in two rows (i.e., cylinder banks)
- Opposed to each other: suited for smaller under hood areas
  Engine Cooling
- Cooling systems
- Air cooling: air is circulated over cooling fins cast into the outside of cylinders and cylinder heads
- Liquid cooling: has cavities in the block and head castings called water jackets
- Water pump pumps coolant through the system
- Coolant mixture is designed to prevent rust and electrolysis: 50% water and

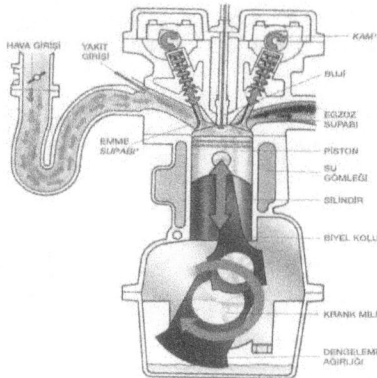

50% anti-freeze

1.Four stroke engine

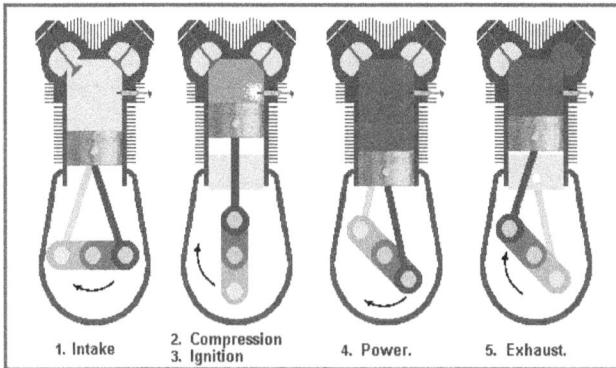

1. Intake   2. Compression 3. Ignition   4. Power.   5. Exhaust.

Figure 6-3 Four-stroke five-event cycle.

- Suction
- Compression
- Power (combustion)
- Exhaust

Firing Order

- Ignition interval
- Interval between power strokes
- Within two turns of the crankshaft, all cylinders fire once
- Firing order: order in which the cylinders fire
- Companion cylinders
- Pairs of cylinders in engines with an even number of cylinders

2 Stroke Engine

- It's called a two-stoke engine because there is a compression stroke and then a combustion stroke.
- In a four-stroke engine, there are separate intake, compression, combustion and exhaust strokes.

Note:

- Mix special two-stroke oil in with the gasoline
- Mix oil in with the fuel to lubricate the crankshaft, connecting rod and cylinder walls
- Note: If you forget to mix in the oil, the engine isn't going to last very long!

Advantage

- Two-stroke engines do not have valves, which simplifies their construction and lowers their weight.
- Two-stroke engines fire once every revolution, while four-stroke engines fire once every other revolution. This gives two-stroke engines a

significant power boost.
- Two-stroke engines can work in any orientation, A standard four-stroke engine may have problems with oil flow unless it is upright
- These advantages make two-stroke engines lighter, simpler and less expensive to manufacture.
- Two-stroke engines also have the potential to pack about twice the power into the same space because there are twice as many power strokes per revolution

Disadvantages
- Two-stroke engines don't last nearly as long as four-stroke engines.
- Two-stroke oil is expensive, You would burn about a 3.7 litres of oil every 1600km if you used a two-stroke engine in a car.
- Two-stroke engines are not fuel efficient, so you would get fewer miles per gallon.
- Two-stroke engines produce a lot of pollution
  1) from the combustion of the oil.
  2) Each time a new charge of air/fuel is loaded into the combustion chamber, part of it leaks out through the exhaust port.

Intake
- As the piston finally bottoms out, the intake port is uncovered. The piston's movement has pressurized the mixture in the crankcase, so it rushes into the cylinder, displacing the remaining exhaust gases and filling the cylinder with a fresh charge of fuel
- Note that in many two-stroke engines that use a cross-flow design, the piston is shaped so that the incoming fuel mixture doesn't simply flow right over the top of the piston and out the exhaust port.

Exhaust
- Fuel and air in the cylinder have been compressed, and when the spark plug fires the mixture ignites. The resulting explosion drives the piston downward. Note that as the piston moves downward, it is compressing the air/fuel mixture in the crankcase. As the piston approaches the bottom of its stroke, the exhaust port is uncovered. The pressure in the cylinder drives most of the exhaust gases out of cylinder, as shown here:

Compression Stroke
- Now the momentum in the crankshaft starts driving the piston back toward the spark plug for the compression stroke. As the air/fuel mixture in the piston is compressed, a vacuum is created in the crankcase. This vacuum opens the reed valve and sucks air/fuel/oil in from the carburetor.
- Reed valves are a type of check valve which restrict the flow of fluids to a single direction, opening and closing under changing pressure on each face

Calorific value of fuel
- The calorific value of a fuel is the quantity of heat produced by its combustion – at constant pressure and under "normal" (standard) conditions (i.e. to 0°C and under a pressure of 1.013 bar).
The calorific value of diesel fuel is roughly 45.5 MJ/kg

Slightly lower than petrol which is 45.8 MJ/kg.
However, diesel fuel is denser than petrol and contains about 15% more energy by volume (roughly 36.9 MJ/litre compared to 33.7 MJ/litre

Valve timing diagram

- In a piston engine, the valve timing is the precise
- Timing of the opening and closing of the valves.
- In an internal combustion engine those are usually poppet valves
- In a steam engine they are usually slide valves or piston valves

Valve timing diagram

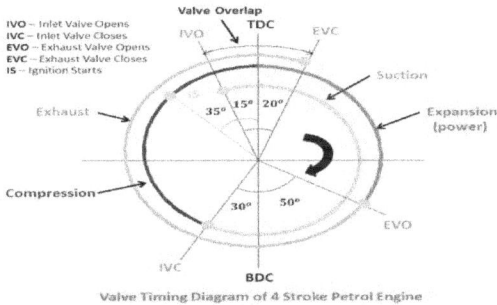

IVO – Inlet Valve Opens
IVC – Inlet Valve Closes
EVO – Exhaust Valve Opens
EVC – Exhaust Valve Closes
IS – Ignition Starts

Valve Timing Diagram of 4 Stroke Petrol Engine

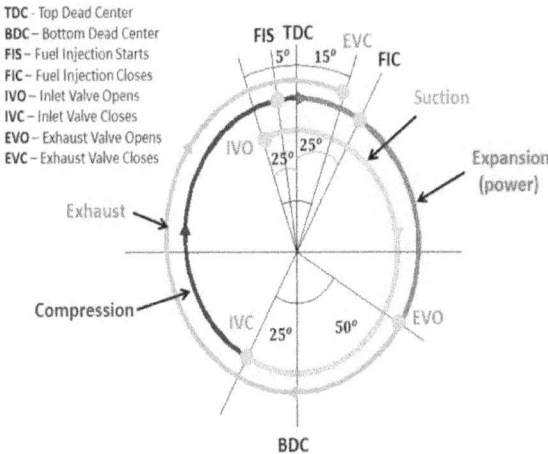

TDC - Top Dead Center
BDC – Bottom Dead Center
FIS – Fuel Injection Starts
FIC – Fuel Injection Closes
IVO – Inlet Valve Opens
IVC – Inlet Valve Closes
EVO – Exhaust Valve Opens
EVC – Exhaust Valve Closes

Valve Timing Diagram of 4 Stroke Diesel Engine

Port Timing Diagram for Two Stroke Petrol Engine
- In the case of two stroke cycle engines the inlet and exhaust valves are not present.

97

- Instead, the slots are cut on the cylinder itself at different elevation and they are called ports.
- There are three ports are present in the two stroke cycle engine.
- 1. Inlet port
- 2. Transfer port
- 3. Exhaust port

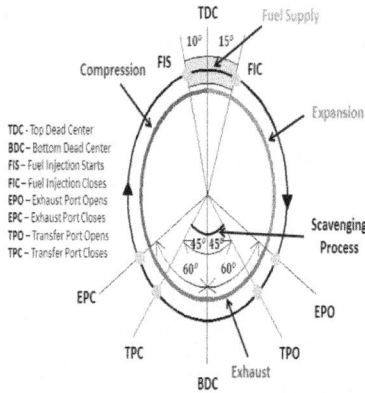

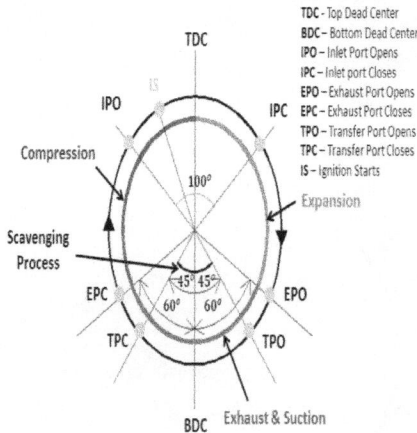

TURBINE ENGINE

The gas turbine engine mounted on most helicopters is made up of a compressor, combustion chamber, turbine, and gear box assembly. The compressor compresses the air, which is then fed into the combustion chamber where atomized fuel is injected into it. The fuel/air mixture is ignited and allowed to expand. This combustion gas is then forced through a series of turbine wheels causing them to turn. These turbine wheels provide power to both the engine compressor and the main rotor system through an output shaft. The combustion gas is finally expelled through an exhaust outlet

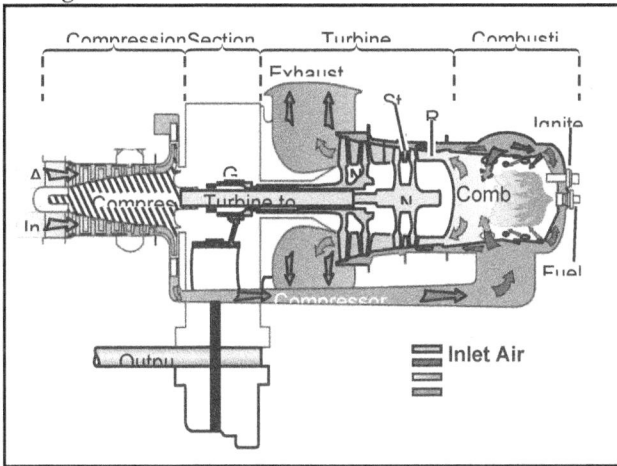

COMPRESSOR

The compressor may consist of an axial compressor, a centrifugal compressor, or both. An axial compressor consists of two main elements, the rotor and the stator. The rotor consists of a number of blades fixed on a rotating spindle and resembles a fan. As the rotor turns, air is drawn rearwards. Stator vanes are arranged in fixed rows between the rotor blades and act as a diffuser at each stage to decrease air velocity and increase air pressure. There may be a number of rows of rotor blades and stator vanes. Each row constitutes a pressure stage, and the number of stages depends on the amount of air and pressure rise required for the particular engine.

A centrifugal compressor consists of an impeller, dif- fuser, and a manifold. The impeller, which is a forged disc with integral blades, rotates at a high speed to draw air in and expel it at an accelerated rate. The air then passes through the diffuser which slows the air down. When the velocity of the air is slowed, static pressure increases, resulting in compressed, high-pres- sure air. The high pressure air then passes through the compressor manifold where it is distributed to the combustion chamber.

COMBUSTION CHAMBER

Unlike a piston engine, the combustion in a turbine engine is continuous. An igniter plug serves only to ignite the fuel/air mixture when starting the engine. Once the fuel/air mixture is ignited, it will continue to burn as long as the fuel/air mixture continues to be present. If there is an interruption of fuel, air, or both, combustion ceases. This is known as a "flame-out," and the engine has to be restarted or re-lit. Some helicopters are equipped with auto-relight, which automatically activates the igniters to start combustion if the engine flames out.

TURBINE

The turbine section consists of a series of turbine wheels that are used to drive the compressor section and the rotor system. The first stage, which is usually referred to as the gas producer or N_1 may consist of one or more turbine wheels. This stage drives the components necessary to complete the turbine cycle making the engine self-sustaining. Common components driven by the N_1 stage are the compressor, oil pump, and fuel pump. The second stage, which may also consist of one or more wheels, is dedicated to driving the main rotor system and accessories from the engine gearbox. This is referred to as the power turbine (N_2 or N_r).

Pulse jet engine

- Inlet diffuser , valve grid loaded with spring , Combustion chamber, spark plug, nozzle
- When certain pressure drop exits across the valve grid it open
- Pressurized air get ignited
- Expands jet through nozzle
- Firing the combustor is intermittent (irregular)
- well suited for low speed
- Cheap engine

Turbo jet engine
Advantage

- Lower frontal area – less drag
- Suitable for long distance , higher altitude and speeds
- Can operate at static condition has compressor
- Reheat can be possible
- Diffuser supports the compressor

Disadvantage

- Propulsive efficiency is less at lower speed
- TSFC is high at low speeds
- Not economical for short range
- Long run way required for lower acceleration
- Sudden decrease in speed is difficult to achieve

Turbo prop engine
Advantage

- Propulsive efficiency is high
- The TSFC based on thrust is low
- High acceleration – shorter run way

- Thrust reversal is possible by varying speed

Disadvantage
- Profile drag – propeller
- Reduction gear arrangement is required
- If the speed increases the efficiency decreases drastically
- High frontal area
- Engine design is complicated

Ram jet engine
Advantage
- Pay load capacity is very high
- Suitable for propelling supersonic missiles
- Less frontal area – less drag
- High mechanical efficiency (less moving parts)
- High temperature and pressure can be employed

Disadvantage
- A starting device is required
- Altitude limitation is there
- TSFC is high
- Nozzle erosion will be more

Pulse jet engine
Advantage
- High pay load capacity
- Simple construction
- Less profile drag
- Mechanical efficiency is high

Disadvantage
- Limited speed
- Limited altitude
- Noise will be - high intermittent combustion
- Nozzle erosion

USE OF PROPELLER for THRUST PRODUCTION

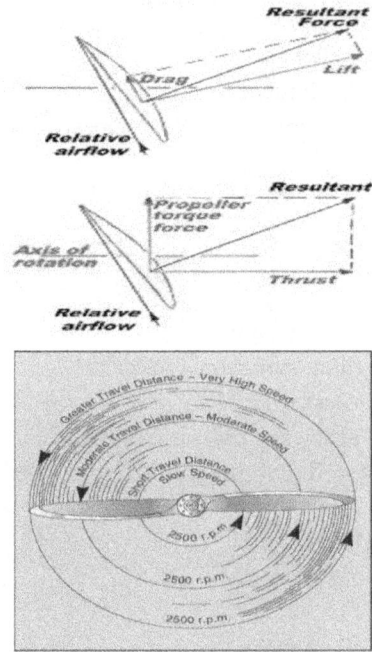

- The cross section of propeller blade is an airfoil.
- As the propeller rotates through the air, it generates lift,
- which becomes thrust as the it is directed forwards rather than vertically upwards as in aircraft wing

- At any RPM, different section of the propeller are at different angles of attack.
- To remedy this, the airfoil sections are varied along the propeller.
- So the propeller is practically twisted along its length, with the root at higher angle of attack.
- the pitch of the propeller blades can be varied in flight.
- propeller that is set parallel to the airflow. This is done usually in order to reduce drag in case of engine failure.
- During normal operation, the blades will not be in feathered position
- In aircraft, propeller pitch is changed with speed,
- with fine pitch at low speeds and strong acceleration (like take off) and a coarse pitch for high speed (cruise).
- In most aircraft, the propeller pitch settings are adjusted automatically by a governor according to requirements.

Types of propeller

- Fixed pitch: The propeller is made in one piece. Only one pitch setting is possible and is usually two blades propeller and is often made of wood or metal.
- Wooden Propellers : Wooden propellers were used almost exclusively on personal and business aircraft prior to World War II
- Metal Propellers: During 1940, solid steel propellers were made for military use.
- Ground adjustable pitch: The pitch setting can be adjusted only with tools on the ground before the engine is running.
- Two-position: A propeller which can have its pitch changed from one position to one other angle by the pilot while in flight.
- Controllable pitch: The pilot can change the pitch of the propeller in flight or while operating the engine by mean of a pitch changing mechanism that may be operated by hydraulically.
- Constant speed : The constant speed propeller utilizes a hydraulically or electrically operated pitch changing mechanism which is controlled by governor
- Full Feathering : A constant speed propeller which has the ability to turn edge to the wind and thereby eliminate drag and wind milling in the event of engine failure
- Reversing : A constant speed propeller which has the ability to assume a negative blade angle and produce a reversing thrust
- Beta Control : A propeller which allows the manual repositioning of the propeller blade angle beyond the normal low pitch stop

Thrust bending force Thrust loads on the blades, in reaction to the force pushing the air backwards, act to bend the blades forward

Centrifugal and aerodynamic twisting forces In the propeller it acts to twist the blades to a fine pitch. The aerodynamic centre of pressure is therefore usually arranged to be slightly forward of its mechanical centreline

Centrifugal force The force felt by the blades acting to pull them away from the hub when turning.

Torque bending force : Air resistance acting against the blades, combined with inertial effects causes propeller blades to bend away from the direction of rotation.

Comparison

- Air-Breathing Systems . Also called *duct propulsion*.
- Vehicle carries own fuel , Use surrounding air (an *oxidizer*) for thrust generation
- Gas turbine engines on aircraft
- Altitude limitation
- Thrust decreases with altitude
- Rate of climb decreases with altitude
- Engine ram drag increases with flight speed
- Flight speed always less than jet velocity
- Reasonable efficiency and flight duration
- Rocket Propulsion
- Vehicle carries own fuel and oxidizer, propellant to generate thrust:
- Can operate outside of the Earth's atmosphere
- Launch vehicles, upper stages, Earth orbiting satellites and interplanetary spacecraft
- No altitude limitation
- Thrust increases slightly with altitude
- Rate of climb increases with altitude
- Engine has no ram drag ; constant thrust with speed
- Flight speed not limited can be greater than jet velocity
- Low efficiency except at extremely high flight speed for small duration

What is propulsion?
- Act of changing the motion of a body.
- Propulsion mechanism provide a force that moves bodies that are initially at rest, changes a velocity, or overcome retarding force when a body is propelled through a medium.
1. Chemical rocket engines
2. Nuclear rocket engine
3. Electrical rocket engine
4. Solar rocket engine

Chemical
1. Liquid propellant rocket engine
2. Solid propellant rocket engine
3. Hybrid propellant rocket engine
- Based on application
    Space , military, weather , booster

- Based on stages
  Single, multi stage
- Based on range
  Short range small
  long range larger

PRINCIPLES OF OPERATION OF ROCKET

- A rocket is like a chamber enclosing a gas under pressure.
- A small opening at one end of the chamber allows the gas to escape
- provides a thrust that propels the rocket in the opposite direction.
- A good example of this is a balloon. Air inside a balloon is compressed by the balloon's rubber wall.
- When the nozzle is released, air escapes through it and the balloon is propelled in the opposite direction.

Rocket engines

- The only known way to meet space-flight velocity requirements is through the use of the rocket in one of its several forms.
- Rocket *thrust* is the reaction force produced by expelling particles at high velocity from a nozzle opening.
- These expelled particles may be solid, liquid, gaseous, or even bundles of radiant energy.
- Because of this fundamental fact, a prime criterion for rating rocket performance is specific impulse, which provides an index of the efficiency with which a rocket uses its supply of propellant or working fluid for thrust production.
- For gaseous working fluids, specific impulse can be increased by (1) attaining higher temperatures in the combustion chamber and (2) increasing the proportion of lighter gases, preferably hydrogen, in the exhaust.

Rocket Propulsion
Principle:

- It consists of combustion chamber and an expanding nozzle.
- The fuel and oxidant, when ignited cause the combustion to proceed at a very fast rate.
- The exhaust gases produce the required propulsive forces.
- In other words propellant gases, that are generated in the CC are expanded in a nozzle to a supersonic velocity. The high velocity gases going out of nozzle produce the thrust and propel the rocket

Liquid propellant rocket engine
Construction

- Liquid oxygen and liquid fuel is stored in different tank separately
- Pre heater is used to heat the fuel and oxidizer
- Nozzle is used to increase the velocity & decreases the pressure of the gases

Working

- Oxidizer and fuel are pumped separately in to a combustion chamber through the control valve
- Since oxidizer and fuel stored at very low temperature they are pre heated with suitable pre heaters
- Then injected in to the combustion chamber & combustion

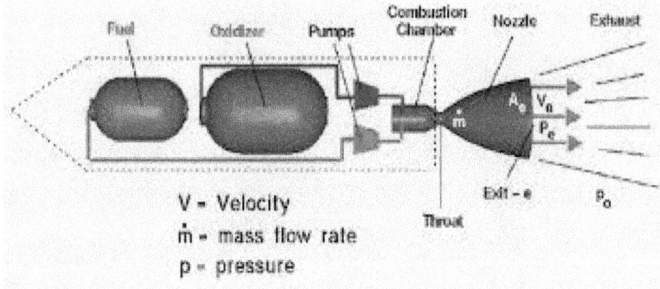

Fuel   Oxidizer   Pumps   Combustion Chamber   Nozzle   Exhaust

A_e V_e P_e m Exit - e P_o Throat

V - Velocity
m - mass flow rate
p - pressure

take place
- The combustion gas allowed to expand through nozzle
- The nozzle , pressure energy is converted in to KE , gas coming out of the unit with very high velocity
- Thrust produced at opposite direction and propels the rocket

Advantage

- Can be reused after recovery
- Combustion is controlled very easily by control valve
- Speed regulation is possible by varying the mixture
- High specific impulse
- More economical for long range operation
- Accidents can be rectified at any stage
- Disadvantages
- Construction is complicated than solid rockets
- Handling problem if the fuel is poisonous or corrosive
- Size and weight of engine is more
- High vibration

- Fuel can exist in liquid form only at low temperature so proper insulation needed

Advantages of liquid propellant
- Engine can be reused after recovery
- More flexible and greater control over thrust
- Aerodynamically and structurally better and safer
- Higher safety
- Regenerative heating
- More economical
- Provide relatively higher thrust than solid propellants.

Disadvantages of liquid propellants
- **Liquid** propellants are difficult to handle and require separate storage tanks.
- They demand a complex engine with pumps and turbo-compressors for feeding to combustion chamber
- Lower density

Properties of liquid propellant
- Propellant should have high CV
- Its density should be high
- It should have low value of vapor pressure and viscosity
- Should have high specific heat and thermal conductivity
- Low Molecular weight
- No corrosive & nor reactive wit engine components
- Should not poisonous
- Easily ignitable
- Cheap and easily available

Properties of liquid propellant
- High calorific value
- High density
- Lower freezing point
- Non-corrosive
- Chemically stable
- They should not be poisonous and hazardous
- Cheap and easily available

SOLID-PROPELLANT ROCKET

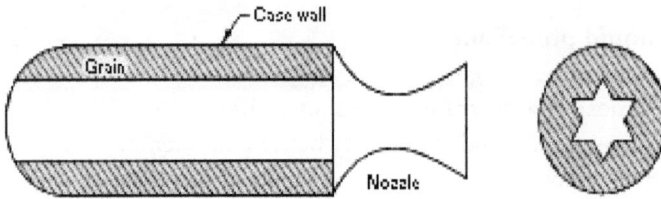

- The propellant grain is firmly cemented to the inside of the metal or plastic case
- This hole, called the perforation, may be shaped in various ways, as star, gear, or other more unusual outlines
- The perforation shape and dimension affects the burning rate or number of pounds of gas generated per second and, thereby, the thrust of the engine.
- After being ignited by a pyrotechnic device, which is usually triggered by an electrical impulse
- The propellant grain burns on the entire inside surface of the perforation.
- The hot combustion gases pass down the grain and are ejected through the nozzle to produce thrust.

Solid propellant rocket engine:
- The propellant to be burned is contained within the combustion chamber or case.
- The solid propellant charges are called the grain and it contains all the chemical elements for complete burning.
- Once ignited, it usually burns smoothly at predetermined rate on all the exposed internal surfaces of grain.
- The resulting hot gases flows through supersonic nozzle, thereby imparting thrust to the vehicle.

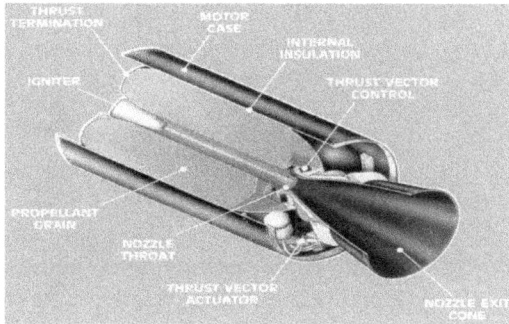

On most turbine assemblies used in helicopters, the first stage and second stage turbines are not mechani- cally connected to each other. Rather, they are mounted on independent shafts and can turn freely with respect to each other. This is referred to as a "free turbine." When the engine is running, the combustion gases pass through the first stage turbine to drive the compressor rotor, and then past the independent second stage tur- bine, which turns the gearbox to drive the output shaft.

CHAPTER 6

HELICOPTER AND ROTARY WING AIRCRAFT

Rotorcraft

Types
•Helicopter
•Cyclogyro/cyclocopter
•Autogyro
•Gyrodyne/gyroplane
•Rotor kite
•Known as rotary wing aircraft
•Lift generated by rotary wings(no fixed wing)
•Several rotor wings mounted on a single rotor mast
•Insomecasesoneormorerotorassemblywillbemountedforbetterlistandma neuvering
•some design includes additional static surfaces for lift, propellers, thrust engines etc.,

Cyclogyro / cyclocopter
Rotor craft rotor is driven by the engine through out the flight
•The blade rotates about the horizontal axis
•Blade parallel to its camber

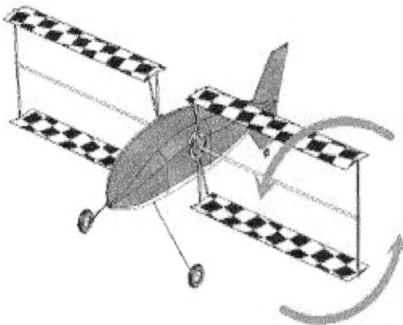

Auto gyro / gyro plane / gyro copter / rotor plane
An autogyro, also known as a gyroplane or gyrocopter,
Is a type of rotorcraft that uses an unpowered rotor in free autorotation

to develop lift.

Forward thrust is provided independently, typically by an engine-driven propeller

All the above type utilize an unpowered rotor driven by aerodynamics forces

Tat rotor will generate lift

An engine powered propeller will be their to produce thrust

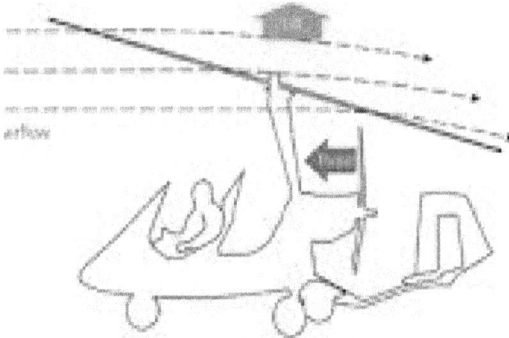

Gyrocopter in autorotation

Whereas a helicopter works by forcing the rotor blades through the air, drawing air from above. The auto gyro rotor blade generates lift in the same way as a glider's wing. By changing the angle of the air as the air moves upwards and backwards relative to the rotor blade

The gyrocopter has a maximum speed of 185 km/h and a cruising speed of 160 km/h. A maximum of 120 meters distance is needed for take-off and only 20 meters for landing. The gyrocopter can fly 500 km without landing or refueling and can stay aloft on its fuel supply for 4 hours.

How a helicopter fly (basics aerodynamics)

Helicopter is a far more complex machine than an aero plane

The fundamental principles of flight are the same. The rotor blades of a helicopter are identical to the wings of an aero plane (when air is blown over them, lift is produced). The crucial difference is that the flow of air is produced by rotating the wings – or rotor blades – rather than by moving the whole aircraft. When the rotor blades start to spin, the air flowing over them produces lift, and this can cause the helicopter to rise into the air. The engine is used to turn the blades, and the turning blades produce the required lift.

How does autorotation work in a helicopter?

Descent and landing. For a helicopter, "autorotation" refers to the descending maneuver in which the engine is disengaged from the main rotor system and the rotor blades are driven solely by the upward flow of air through the rotor. This maneuver is used to land from a hover without using the engine. This would normally occur because the engine or tail rotor failed. The name "hovering autorotation" is really a misleading term, because the helicopter actually never enters autorotation. Instead, the inertia of the spinning rotor system is used to produce thrust. The rotor system of a typical helicopter stores a fair amount of kinetic energy. This energy can be extracted as thrust by allowing the rotor RPM to decrease, giving up the stored energy. There is only a limited amount of energy available, and this determines the maximum height from which the helicopter can be landed without damage

Helicopters come in many sizes and shapes, but most share the same major components. These components include a cabin where the **payload** and crew are carried; an airframe, which houses the various components, or where components are attached; a power plant or engine;

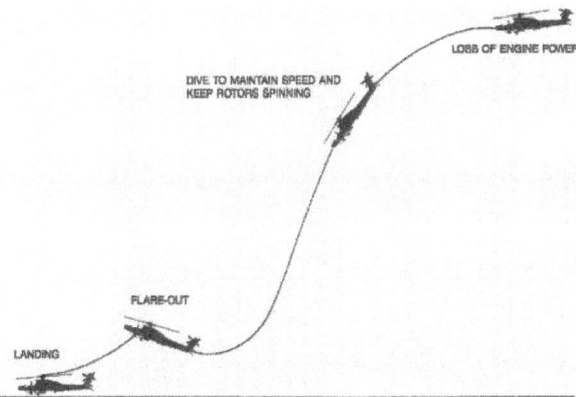

LOSS OF ENGINE POWER

DIVE TO MAINTAIN SPEED AND
KEEP ROTORS SPINNING

FLARE-OUT

LANDING

and a transmission, which, among other things, takes the power from the engine and transmits it to the main rotor, which provides the aerodynamic forces that make the helicopter fly. Then, to keep the helicopter from turning due to **torque**, there must be some type of anti torque system. Finally there is the landing gear, which could be skids, wheels, skis, or floats. This chapter is an introduction to these

THE MAIN ROTOR SYSTEM

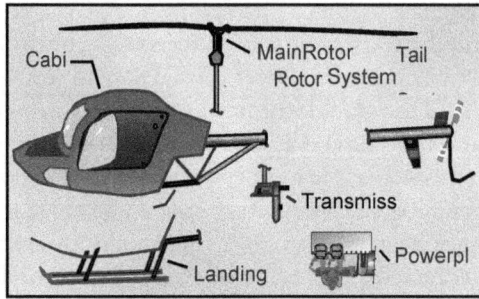

The rotor system found on helicopters can consist of a single main rotor or dual rotors. With most dual rotors, the rotor s turn in opposite directions so the torque from one rotor is opposed by the torque of the other. This cancels the turning tendencies. In general, a rotor system can be classified as either fully articulated, semi rigid, or rigid. There are variations and combinations of these systems, which will be discussed in greater detail in Chapter 5—Helicopter Systems.

FULLY ARTICULATED ROTOR SYSTEM

A fully articulated rotor system usually consists of three or more rotor blades. The blades are allowed to **flap, feather**, and **lead or lag** independently of each other. Each rotor blade is attached to the rotor hub by a horizontal hinge, called the flapping hinge, which permits the blades to flap up and down. Each blade can move up and down independently of the others. The flapping hinge may be located at varying distances from the rotor hub, and there may be more than one. The position is chosen by each manufacturer, primarily with regard to stability and control.

Each rotor blade is also attached to the hub by a vertical hinge, called a drag or lag hinge, that permits each blade, independently of the others, to move back and forth in the plane of the rotor disc. Dampers are normally incorporated in the design of this type of rotor system to prevent excessive motion about the drag hinge. The purpose of the drag hinge and dampers is to absorb the acceleration and deceleration of the rotor blades.

The blades of a fully articulated rotor can also be feathered, or rotated about their span wise axis. To put it more simply, feathering means the changing of the pitch angle of the rotor blades.

rotor system. Other types absorb the shocks by the bending of the skid attachment arms. Landing skids may be fitted with replaceable heavy- duty skid shoes to protect them from excessive wear and tear.

Helicopters can also be equipped with floats for water operations, or skis for landing on snow or soft terrain. Wheels are another type of landing gear. They may be in a tricycle or four point configuration. Normally, the nose or tail gear is free to swivel as the helicopter is taxied on the ground.

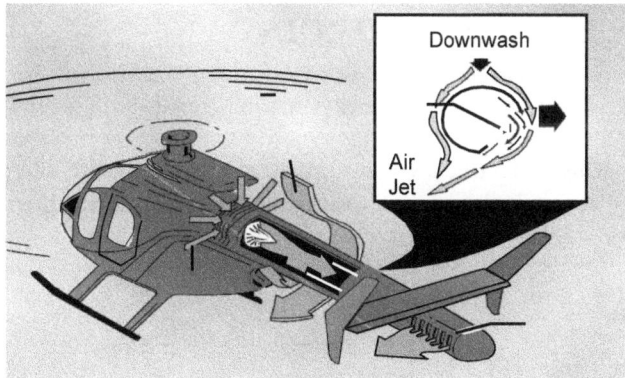

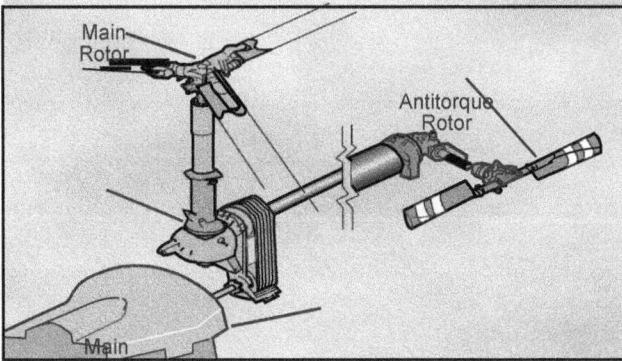

POWERPLANT

A typical small helicopter has a reciprocating engine, which is mounted on the airframe. The engine can be mounted horizontally or vertically with the transmission supplying the power to the vertical main rotor shaft.

Another engine type is the gas turbine. This engine is used in most medium to heavy lift helicopters due to its

large horsepower output. The engine drives the main transmission, which then transfers power directly to the main rotor system, as well as the tail rotor.

FLIGHT CONTROLS

When you begin flying a helicopter, you will use four basic   flight controls. They are the cyclic pitch control; the collective pitch control; the throttle, which is usually a twist grip control located on the end of the collective lever; and the anti torque pedals. The collective and cyclic controls the pitch of the main rotor blades. The function of these controls will be explained in detail in Chapter 4—Flight Controls.

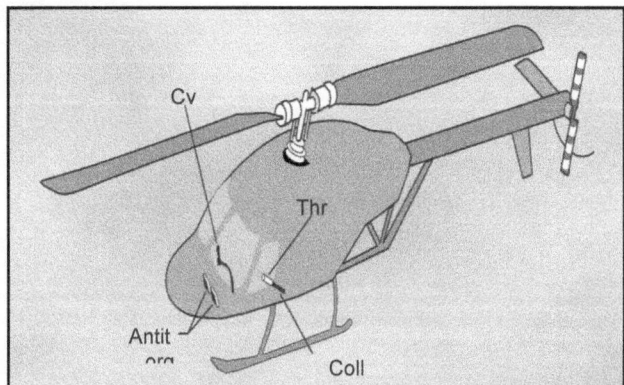

There are four forces acting on a helicopter in flight. They are lift, weight, thrust, and drag. Lift is the upward force created by the effect of air flow as it passes around an airfoil. Weight opposes lift and is caused by the downward pull of gravity. Thrust is the force that propels the helicopter through the air. Opposing lift and thrust is drag, which is the retarding force created by development of lift and the movement of an object through the air.

Symmetrical blades are very stable, which helps keep blade twisting and flight control loads to a minimum. This stability is achieved by keeping the center of pressure virtually unchanged as the angle of attack changes. Center of pressure is the imaginary point on the chord line where the resultant of all aero- dynamic forces are considered to be concentrated.

AIRFOIL

Before beginning the discussion of lift, you need to be aware of certain aerodynamic terms that describe an airfoil and the interaction of the airflow around it.

An airfoil is any surface, such as an airplane wing or a helicopter rotor blade, which provides aerodynamic force when it interacts with a moving stream of air. Although there are many different rotor blade airfoil designs, in most helicopter flight conditions, all airfoils perform in the same manner.

Engineers of the first helicopters designed relatively thick airfoils for their structural characteristics. Because the rotor blades were very long and slender, it was necessary to incorporate more structural rigidity into them. This prevented excessive blade droop when the rotor system was idle, and minimized blade twist- ing while in flight. The airfoils were also designed to be symmetrical, which means they had the same camber (curvature) on both the upper and lower surfaces.

Today, designers use thinner airfoils and obtain the required rigidity by using composite materials. In addition, airfoils are asymmetrical in design, meaning the upper and lower surface do not have the same camber. Normally these airfoils would not be as stable, but this can be corrected by bending the trailing edge to produce the same characteristics as symmetrical airfoils. This is called "reflexing." Using this type of rotor blade allows the rotor system to operate at higher forward speeds.

One of the reasons an asymmetrical rotor blade is not as stable is that the center of pressure changes with changes in angle of attack. When the center of pressure lifting force is behind the pivot point on a rotor blade , it tends to cause the rotor disc to pitch up. As the angle of attack increases, the center of pressure moves forward. If it moves ahead of the pivot point, the pitch of the rotor disc decreases. Since the angle of attack of the rotor blades is constantly changing during each cycle of rotation, the blades tend to flap, feather, lead, and lag to a greater degree.

When referring to an airfoil, the span is the distance from the rotor hub to the blade tip. Blade twist refers to a changing chord line from the blade root to the tip.

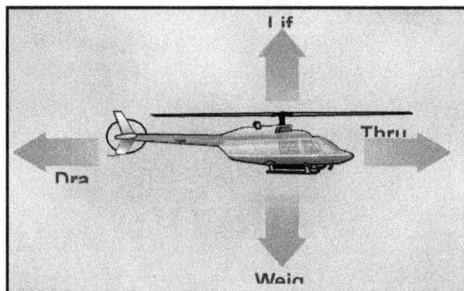

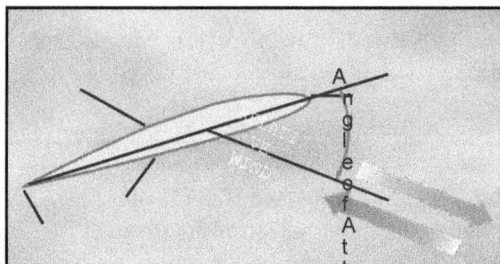

Twisting a rotor blade causes it to produce a more even amount of lift along its span. This is necessary because rotational velocity increases toward the blade tip. The leading edge is the first part of the airfoil to meet the oncoming air. [Figure 2-3] The trailing edge is the aft portion where the airflow over the upper surface joins the airflow under the lower surface. The chord line is an imaginary straight line drawn from the leading to the trailing edge. The camber is the curvature of the air- foil's upper and lower surfaces. The relative wind is the wind moving past the airfoil. The direction of this wind is relative to the attitude, or position, of the airfoil and is always parallel, equal, and opposite in direction to the flight path of the airfoil. The angle of attack is the angle between the blade chord line and the direction of the relative wind.

RELATIVE WIND

Relative wind is created by the motion of an airfoil through the air, by the motion of air past an airfoil, or by a combination of the two. Relative wind may be affected by several factors, including the rotation of the rotor blades, horizontal movement of the helicopter, flapping of the rotor blades, and wind speed and direction.

For a helicopter, the relative wind is the flow of air with respect to the rotor blades. If the rotor is stopped, wind blowing over the blades creates a relative wind. When the helicopter is hovering in a no-wind condition, relative wind is created by the motion of the rotor blades through the air. If the helicopter is hovering in a wind, the relative wind is a combination of the wind and the motion of the rotor blades through the air. When the helicopter is in forward flight, the relative wind is a combination of the rotation of the rotor blades and the forward speed of the helicopter.

BLADE PITCH ANGLE

The pitch angle of a rotor blade is the angle between its chord line and the reference plane containing the rotor hub. You control the pitch angle of the blades with the flight controls. The collective pitch changes each rotor blade an equal amount of pitch no matter where it is located in the plane of rotation (rotor disc) and is used to change rotor thrust. The cyclic pitch control changes the pitch of each blade as a function of where it is in the plane of rotation. This allows for trimming the helicopter in **pitch** and **roll** during forward flight and for maneuvering in all flight conditions.

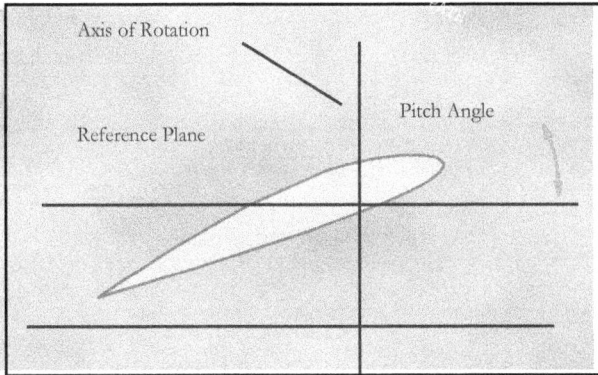

ANGLE OF ATTACK

When the angle of attack is increased, air flowing over the airfoil is diverted over a greater distance, resulting in an increase of air velocity and more lift. As angle of attack is increased further, It becomes more difficult for air to flow smoothy across the top of the airfoil. At this point the air flow begins to separate from the airfoil and enters a burbling or turbulent pattern. The turbulence results in a large increase in drag and loss of lift in the area where it is taking place. Increasing the angle of attack increases lift until the critical angle of attack is reached. Any increase in the angle of attack beyond this point produces a stall and a rapid decrease in lift.

Angle of attack should not be confused with pitch angle. Pitch angle is determined by the direction of the relative wind. You can, however, change the angle of attack by changing the pitch angle through the use of the flight controls. If the pitch angle is increased, the angle of attack is increased, if the pitch angle is reduced, the angle of attack is reduced.

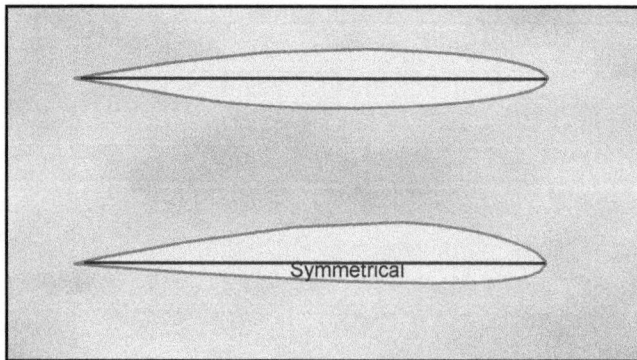

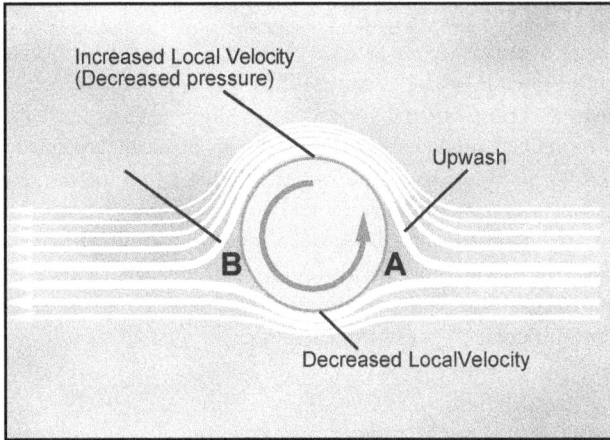

LIFT AND MAGNUS EFFECT

The explanation of lift can best be explained by looking at a cylinder rotating in an air stream. The local velocity near the cylinder is composed of the airstream velocity and the cylinder's rotational velocity, which decreases with distance from the cylinder. On a cylinder, which is rotating in such a way that the top surface area is rotating in the same direction as the airflow, the local velocity at the surface is high on top and low on the bottom.

As shown in , at point "A," a stagnation point exists where the air streamline that impinge on the sur face splits ;some air goes over and some under. Another stagnation point exists at "B," where the two air streams rejoin and resume at identical velocities. We

Now have up wash ahead of the rotating cylinder and downwash at the rear.

The difference in surface velocity accounts for a difference in pressure, with the pressure being lower on the top than the bottom. This low pressure area produces an upward force known as the "Magnus Effect." This mechanically induced circulation illustrates the relationship between circulation and lift.

An airfoil with a positive angle of attack develops air circulation as its sharp trailing edge forces the rear stagnation point to be aft of the trailing edge, while the front stagnation point is below the leading edge.

BERNOULLI'S PRINCIPLE

Air flowing over the top surface accelerates. The airfoil is now subjected to Bernoulli's Principle or the "venturi effect."As air velocity increases through the constricted portion of a venturi tube, the pressure decreases.

The upper half of the venturi tube can be replaced by layers of undisturbed air. Thus, as air flows over the upper surface of an airfoil, the camber of the airfoil causes an increase in the speed of the airflow. The increased speed of airflow results in a decrease in pressure on the upper surface of the airfoil. At the same time, air flows along the lower surface of the airfoil, building up pressure. The combination of decreased pressure on the upper surface and increased pressure on the lower surface results in an upward force.

As angle of attack is increased, the production of lift is increased. More up wash is created ahead of the airfoil as the leading edge stagnation point moves under the leading edge, and more downwash is created aft of the trailing edge. Total lift now being produced is perpendicular to relative wind. In summary, the production of lift is based upon the airfoil creating circulation in the airstream (Magnus Effect) and creating differential pressure on the airfoil (Bernoulli's Principle).

NEWTON'S THIRD LAW OF MOTION

Additional lift is provided by the rotor blade's lower surface as air striking the underside is deflected downward. According to Newton's Third Law of Motion, "for every action there is an equal and opposite reaction,"

the air that is deflected downward also produces an upward (lifting) reaction. Since air is much like water, the explanation for this source of lift may be compared to the planning effect of skis on water. The lift which supports the water skis (and the skier) is the force caused by the impact pres- sure and the deflection of water from the lower surfaces of the skis.

Under most flying conditions, the impact pressure and the deflection of air from the lower surface of the rotor blade provides a comparatively small percentage of the total lift. The majority of lift is the result of decreased pressure above the blade, rather than the increased pressure below it.

WEIGHT

Normally, weight is thought of as being a known, fixed value, such as the weight of the helicopter, fuel, and occupants. To lift the helicopter off the ground vertically, the rotor system must generate enough lift to overcome or offset the total weight of the helicopter and its occupants. This is accomplished by increasing the pitch angle of the main rotor blades.

The weight of the helicopter can also be influenced by aerodynamic loads. When you bank a helicopter while maintaining a constant altitude, the "G" load or load factor increases. Load factor is the ratio of the loads up- ported by the main rotor system to the actual weight of the helicopter and its contents. In **steady-state flight**, the helicopter has a load factor of one , which means the main rotor system is supporting the actual total weight of the helicopter. If you increase the bank angle to 60°, while still maintaining a constant altitude, the load factor increases to two. In this case, the main rotor system has to supp or twice the weight of the helicopter and its contents.

Disc loading of a helicopter is the ratio of weight to the total main rotor disc area, and is determined by dividing the total helicopter weight by the rotor disc area, which is the area swept by the blades of a rotor. Disc area can be found by using the span of one rotor blade as the radius of a circle and then determining the area the blades encompass during a complete rotation. As the helicopter is maneuvered, disc loading changes. The higher the loading, the more power you need to maintain rotor speed.

DRAG

The force that resists the movement of a helicopter through the air and is produced when lift is developed is called drag. Drag always acts parallel to the relative wind. Total drag is composed of three types of drag: profile, induced, and parasite.

PROFILE DRAG

Profile drag develops from the frictional resistance of the blades passing through the air. It does not change significantly with the airfoil's angle of attack, but increases moderately when airspeed increases. Profile drag is composed of form drag and skin friction.

THRUST

Thrust, like lift, is generated by the rotation of the main rotor system. In a helicopter, thrust can be for- ward, rearward, sideward, or vertical. The resultant of lift and thrust determines the direction of movement of the helicopter.

The solidity ratio is the ratio of the total rotor blade area, which is the combined area of all the main rotor blades, to the total rotor disc area. This ratio provides a means to measure the potential for a rotor system to provide thrust.

The tail rotor also produces thrust. The amount of thrust is variable through the use of the anti torque pedals and is used to control the helicopter's **yaw**.

Form drag results from the turbulent wake caused by the separation of airflow from the surface of a structure. The amount of drag is related to both the size and shape of the structure that protrudes into the relative wind.

Skin friction is caused by surface roughness. Even though the surface appears smooth, it may be quite rough when viewed under a microscope. A thin layer of air clings to the rough surface and creates small eddies that contribute to drag.

INDUCED DRAG

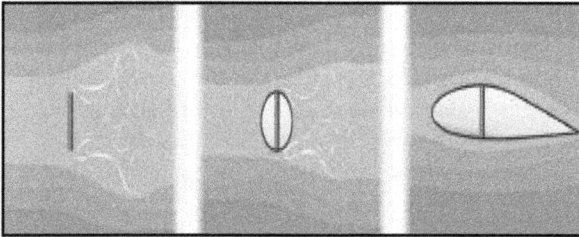

Induced drag is generated by the airflow circulation around the rotor blade as it creates lift. The high-pres- sure area beneath the blade joins the low-pressure air above the blade at the trailing edge and at the rotor tips. This causes a spiral, or vortex, which trails behind each blade whenever lift is being produced. These vortices deflect the airstream downward in the vicinity of the blade, creating an increase in downwash. Therefore, the blade operates in an average relative wind that is inclined downward and rearward near the blade. Because the lift produced by the blade is perpendicular to the relative wind, the lift is inclined aft by the same amount. The component of lift that is acting in a rear- ward direction is induced drag with increasing airspeed, parasite drag is the major cause of drag at higher airspeeds. Parasite drag varies with the square of the velocity. Doubling the airspeed increases the parasite drag four times.

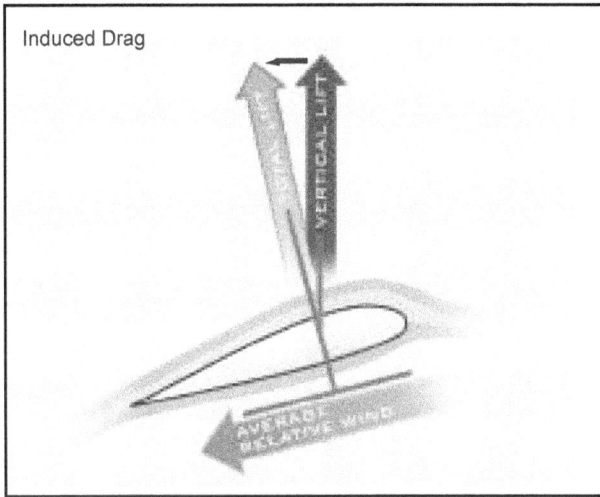

Induced Drag

TOTAL DRAG

Total drag for a helicopter is the sum of all three drag forces. As airspeed increases, parasite drag increases, while induced drag decreases. Profile drag remains relatively constant throughout the speed range with some increase at higher airspeeds. Combining all drag forces results in a total drag curve. The low point on the total drag curve shows the airspeed at which drag is minimized. This is the point where the lift-to-drag ratio is greatest and is referred to as L/Dmax. At this speed, the total lift capacity of the helicopter, when compared to the total drag of the helicopter, is most favorable. This is important in helicopter performance.

As the air pressure differential increases with an increase in angle of attack, stronger vortices form, and induced drag increases. Since the blade's angle of attack is usually lower at higher airspeeds, and higher at low speeds, induced drag decreases as airspeed increases and increases as airspeed decreases. Induced drag is the major cause of drag at lower airspeeds.

PARASITE DRAG

Parasite drag is present any time the helicopter is moving through the air. This type of drag increases with air speed. Non lifting components of the helicopter, such as the cabin, rotor mast, tail, and landing gear, contribute to parasite drag. Any loss of momentum by the airstream, due to such things as openings for engine cooling, creates additional parasite drag. Because of its rapid increase Once a helicopter leaves the ground, it Is acted up on by the four aerodynamic forces. In this chapter, we will examine these forces as they relate to flight maneuvers.

POWERED FLIGHT

In powered flight (hovering, vertical, forward, side- ward, or rearward), the total lift and thrust forces of a rotor are perpendicular to the tip path plane or plane of rotation of the rotor.

HOVERING FLIGHT

For standardization purposes, this discussion assumes a stationary hover in a no-wind condition. During hovering flight, a helicopter maintains a constant position over a selected point, usually a few feet above the ground. For a helicopter to hover, the lift and thrust produced by the rotor system act straight up and must equal the weight and drag, which act straight down. While hovering, you can change the amount of main rotor thrust to maintain the desired hovering altitude. This is done by changing the angle of attack of the main rotor blades and by varying power, as needed. In this case, thrust acts in the same vertical direction as lift.

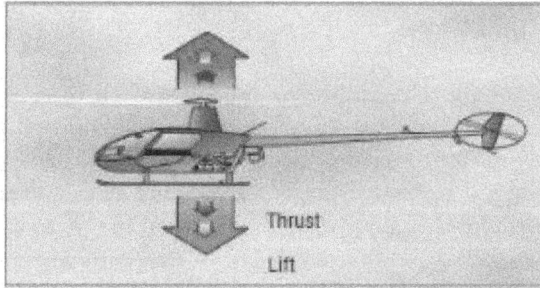

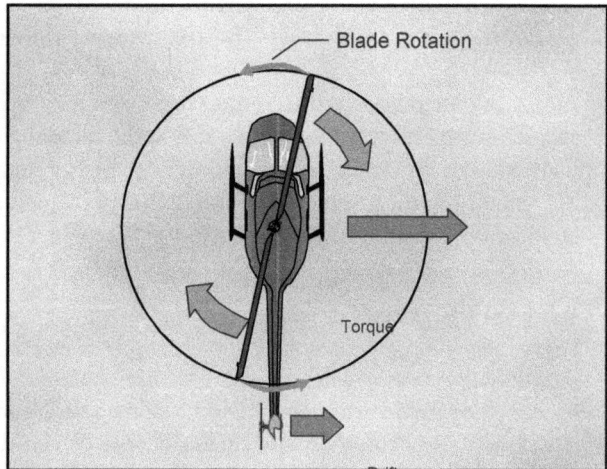

The weight that must be supported is the total weight of the helicopter and its occupants. If the amount of thrust is greater than the actual weight, the helicopter gains altitude; if thrust is less than weight, the helicopter loses altitude.

The drag of a hovering helicopter is mainly induced drag incurred while the blades are producing lift. There is, however, some profile drag on the blades as they rotate through the air. Throughout the rest of this discussion, the term "drag" includes both induced and profile drag.

An important consequence of producing thrust is torque. As stated before, for every action there is an equal and opposite reaction. Therefore, as the engine turns the main rotor system in a counterclockwise direction, the helicopter fuselage turns clockwise. The amount of torque is directly related to the amount of engine power being used to turn the main rotor system. Remember, as power changes, torque changes.

To counteract this torque-induced turning tendency, an anti torque rotor or tail rotor is incorporated into most helicopter designs. You can vary the amount of thrust produced by the tail rotor in relation to the amount of torque produced by the engine. As the engine supplies more power, the tail rotor must produce more thrust. This is done through the use of anti torque pedals.

TRANSLATING TENDENCY OR DRIFT

During hovering flight, a single main rotor helicopter tends to drift in the same direction as anti torque rotor thrust. This drifting tendency is called translating tendency

To counteract this drift, one or more of the following features may be used:

- The main transmission is mounted so that the rotor mast is rigged for the tip path plane to have a built- in tilt opposite tail thrust, thus producing a small sideward thrust.
- Flight control rigging is designed so that the rotor disc is tilted slightly opposite tail rotor thrust when the cyclic is centered.
- The cyclic pitch control system is designed so that the rotor disc tilts slightly opposite tail rotor thrust when in a hover.

Counteracting translating tendency, in a helicopter with a counterclockwise main rotor system, causes the left skid to hang lower while hovering. The opposite is true for rotor systems turning clockwise when viewed from a bove.

PENDULAR ACTION

Since the fuselage of the helicopter, with a single main rotor, is suspended from a single point and has consider- able mass, it is free to oscillate either longitudinally or laterally in the same way as a pendulum. This pendulum action can be exaggerated by over controlling; therefore, control movements should be smooth and not exaggerated. Greater the centrifugal force. This force gives the rotor blades their rigidity and , in turn, the strength to support the weight of the helicopter. The centrifugal force generated determines the maximum operating rotor R.P.M. due to structural limitations on the main rotor system.

As a vertical takeoff is made, two major forces are acting at the same time—centrifugal force acting outward and perpendicular to the rotor mast, and lift acting up ward and parallel to the mast. The result of these two forces is that the blades assume a conical path instead of remaining in the plane perpendicular to the mast.

CORIOLIS EFFECT

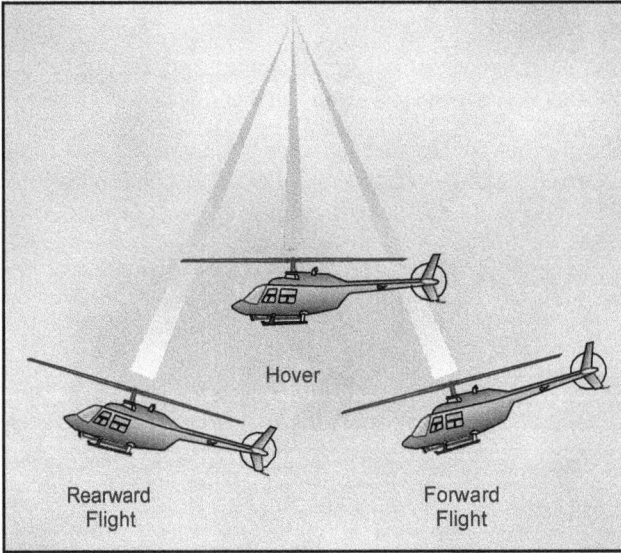

Hover

Rearward
Flight

Forward
Flight

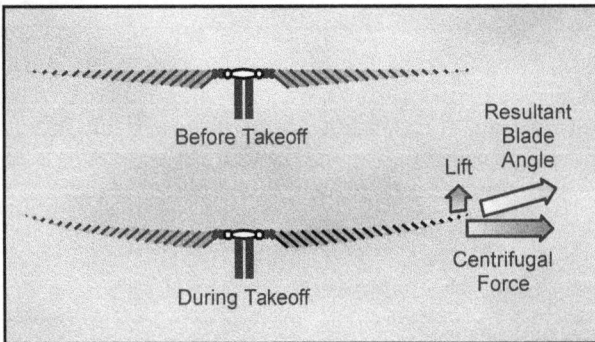

Before Takeoff

During Takeoff

Resultant
Blade
Angle

Lift

Centrifugal
Force

(LAW OF CONSERVATION OF ANGULAR MOMENTUM)

Coriolis Effect, which is sometimes referred to as conservation of angular momentum, might be compared to spinning skaters. When they extend their arms, their rotation slows down because the center of mass moves farther from the axis of rotation. When their arms are retracted, the rotation speeds up because the center of mass moves closer to the axis of rotation.

When a rotor blade flaps upward, the center of mass of that blade moves closer to the axis of rotation and blade acceleration takes place in order to conserve angular momentum. Conversely, when that blade flaps downward, its center of mass moves further from the axis

CONING

In order for a helicopter to generate lift, the rotor blades must be turning. This creates a relative wind that is opposite the direction of rotor system rotation. The rotation of the rotor system creates **centrifugal force** (inertia),which tends to pull the blades straight outward from the main rotor hub. The faster the rotation, the

Rotation and blade deceleration takes place. Keep in mind that due to coning, a rotor blade will not flap below a plane passing through the rotor hub and perpendicular to the axis of rotation. The acceleration and deceleration actions of the rotor blades are absorbed by either dampers or the blade structure itself, depend- ing upon the design of the rotor system. Subject to Coriolis Effect comparable to that of a fully articulated system.

Two-bladed rotor systems are normally subject to Coriolis Effect to a much lesser degree than are articulated rotor systems since the blades are generally "under slung" with respect to the rotor hub, and the change in the distance of the center of mass from the axis of rotation is small. The hunting action is absorbed by the blades through bending. If a two-bladed rotor system is not "under slung," it will be

GROUND EFFECT

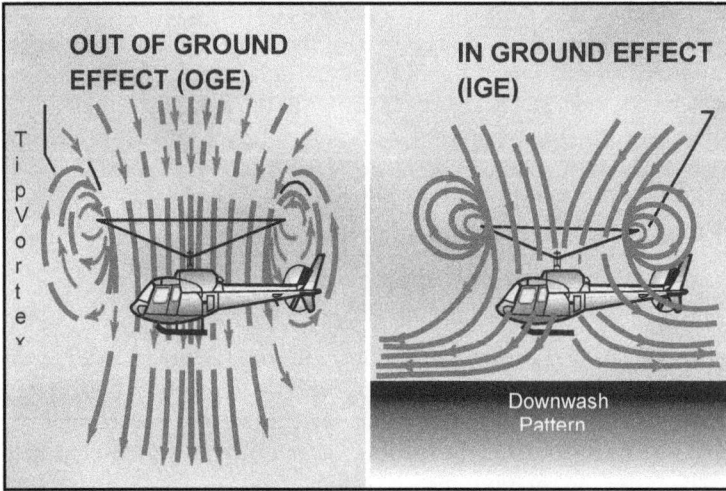

When hovering near the ground, a phenomenon known as ground effect takes place. This effect usually occurs less than one rotor diameter above the surface. As the induced air flow through the rotor disc is reduced by the surface friction, the lift vector increases. This allows a lower rotor blade angle for the same amount of lift, which reduces induced drag. Ground effect also restricts the generation of blade tip vortices due to the downward and outward airflow making a larger portion of the blade produce lift. When the heli- copter gains altitude vertically, with no forward air- speed, induced airflow is no longer restricted, and the blade tip vortices increase with the decrease in outward airflow. As a result, drag increases which means a higher pitch angle, and more power is needed to move the air down through the rotor.

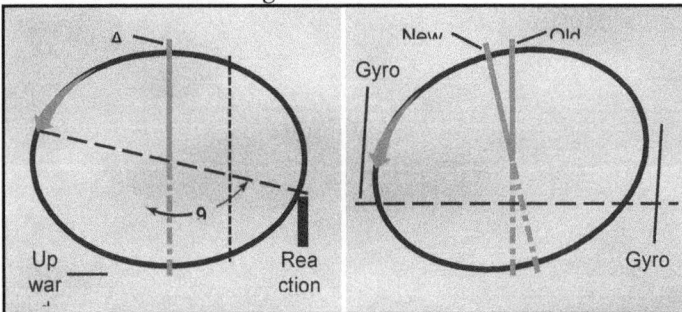

Ground effect is at its maximum in an wind condition over a firm, smooth surface. Tall grass, rough terrain, revetments, and water surfaces alter the air flow pattern, causing an increase in rotor tip vortices. Object when a force is applied to this object. This action occurs approximately 90° in the direction of rotation from the point where the force is applied.

Let us look at a two-bladed rotor system to see how gyroscopic precession affects the movement of the tip- path plane. Moving the cyclic pitch control increases the angle of attack of one rotor blade with the result that a greater lifting force is applied at that point in the plane of rotation. This same control movement simultaneously decreases the angle of attack of the other blade the same amount, thus decreasing the lifting force applied at that point in the plane of rotation. The blade with the increased angle of attack tends to flap up; the blade with the decreased angle of attack tends to flap down. Because the rotor disk acts like a gyro, the blades reach maximum deflection at a point approximately 90° later in the plane of rotation. As shown in figure 3-9, the retreating blade angle of attack is increased and the advancing blade angle of attack is decreased resulting in a tipping forward of the tip-path plane, since maximum deflection takes place 90° later when the blades are at the rear and front, respectively.

In a rotor system using three or more blades, the movement of the cyclic pitch control changes the angle of attack of each blade an appropriate amount so that the end result is the same.

VERTICAL FLIGHT

Hovering is actually an element of vertical flight. Increasing the angle of attack of the rotor blades (pitch) while their velocity remains constant generates additional vertical lift and thrust and the helicopter ascends. Decreasing the pitch causes the helicopter to descend. In a no wind condition when lift and thrust are less than weight and drag, the helicopter descends vertically. If lift and thrust are greater than weight and drag, the helicopter ascends vertically.

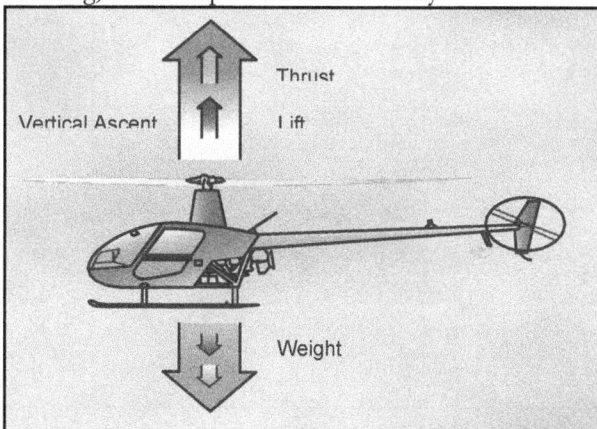

FORWARD FLIGHT

In or during forward flight, the tip path plane is tilted forward, thus tilting the total lift thrust force forward from the vertical. This resultant lift thrust force can be resolved in to two components—lift acting vertically upward and thrust acting horizontally in the direction of flight. In addition to lift and thrust, there is weight (the downward acting force) and drag (the rear ward acting or retarding force of inertia and wind resistance).

In straight-and-level, un accelerated forward flight, lift equals weight and thrust equals drag (straight-and-level flight is flight with a constant heading an data constant altitude). If lift exceeds weight, the helicopter climbs; if lift is less than weight, the helicopter descends. If thrust exceeds drag, the helicopter speeds up; if thrust is less than drag, it slows down.

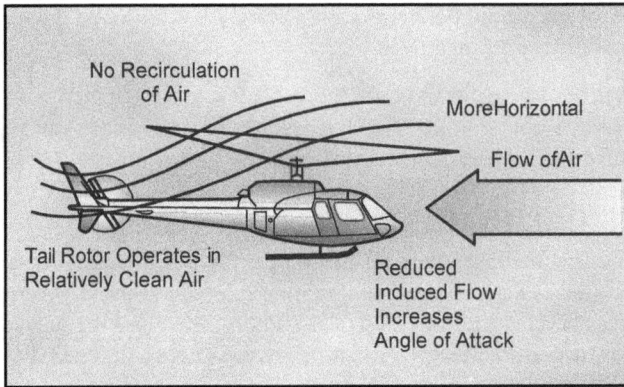

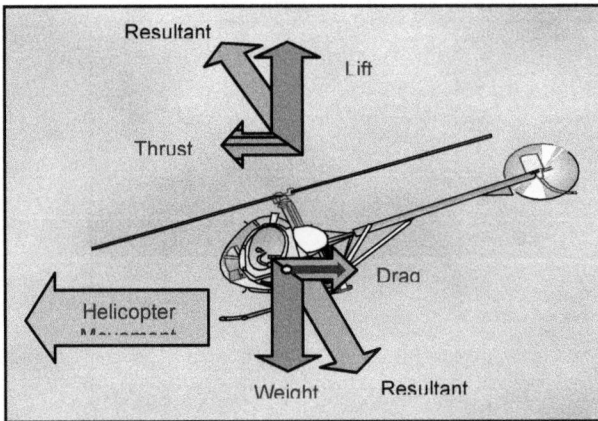

When a single-rotor helicopter flies through translational lift, the air flowing through the main rotor and over the tail rotor becomes less turbulent and more aerodynamically efficient. As the tail rotor efficiency improves, more thrust is produced causing the aircraft to yaw left in a counterclockwise rotor system. It will be necessary to use right torque pedal to correct for this tendency on takeoff. Also, if no corrections are made, the nose rises or pitches up, and rolls to the right. This is caused by combined effects of dissymmetry of lift and transverse flow effect, and is corrected with cyclic control.

Translational lift is also present in a stationary hover if the wind speed is approximately 16 to 24 knots. In normal operations, always utilize the benefit of translational lift, especially if maximum performance is needed.

INDUCED FLOW

As the rotor blades rotate they generate what is called rotational relative wind. This airflow is characterized as flowing parallel and opposite the rotor's plane of rotation and striking perpendicular to the rotor blade's leading edge. This rotational relative wind is used to generate lift. As rotor blades produce lift, air is accelerated over the foil and projected downward. Anytime a helicopter is producing lift, it moves large masses of air vertically and down through the rotor system. This downwash or induced flow can significantly change the efficiency of the rotor system. Rotational relative wind combines with induced flow to form the resultant relative wind. As induced flow increases, resultant relative wind becomes less horizontal. Since angle of attack is determined by measuring the difference between the chord line and the resultant relative wind, as the resultant relative wind becomes less horizontal, angle of attack decreases.

TRANSVERSE FLOW EFFECT

As the helicopter accelerates in forward flight, induced flow drops to near zero at the forward disc area and increases at the aft disc area. This increases the angle of attack at the front disc area causing the rotor blade to flap up, and reduces angle of attack at the aft disc area causing the rotor blade to flap down. Because the rotor acts like a gyro, maximum displacement occurs 90° in the direction of rotation. The result is a tendency for the helicopter to roll slightly to the right as it accelerates through approximately 20 knots or if the head wind is approximately 20knots.

You can recognize transverse flow effect because of increased vibrations of the helicopter at airspeeds just below effective translational lift on takeoff and after passing through effective translational lift during landing. To counteract transverse flow effect, a cyclic input needs to be made.

DISSYMMETRY OF LIFT

When the helicopter moves through the air, the relative airflow through the main rotor disc is different on the advancing side than on the retreating side. The relative wind encountered by the advancing blade is increased by the forward speed of the helicopter, while the relative wind speed acting on the retreating blade is reduced by the helicopter's forward airspeed. Therefore, as a result of the relative wind speed, the advancing blade side of the rotor disc produces more lift than the retreating blade side. This situation is defined as dissymmetry of lift.

If this condition was allowed to exist, a helicopter with a counter clock wise main rotor blade rotation would roll to the left because of the difference in lift. In reality, the main rotor blades flap and feather automatically to equalize lift across the rotor disc. Articulated rotor systems, usually with three or more blades, incorporate a horizontal hinge (flapping hinge) to allow the individual rotor blades to move, or flap up and down as they rotate. A semi rigid rotor system (two blades) utilizes a teetering hinge, which allows the blades to flap as a unit. When one blade flaps up, the other flaps down.

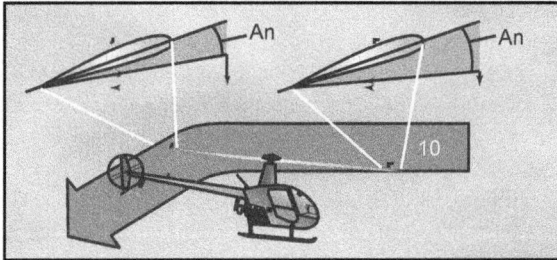

As the rotor blade reaches the advancing side of the rotor disc (A), it reaches its maximum up flap velocity. When the blade flaps upward, the angle between the chord line and the resultant relative wind decreases. This decreases the angle of attack,

Which reduces the amount of lift produced by the blade. At position (C) the rotor blade is now at its maximum down flapping velocity. Due to down flapping, the angle between the chord line and the resultant relative wind increases. This increases the angle of attack and thus the amount of lift produced by the blade.

The combination of blade flapping and low relative wind acting on the retreating blade normally limits the maximum forward speed of a helicopter. At a high forward speed, the retreating blade stalls because of a high angle of attack and slow relative wind speed. This situation is called retreating blade stall and is evidenced by a nose pitch up, vibration, and a rolling tendency—usually to the left in helicopters with counterclockwise blade rotation.

You can avoid retreating blade stall by not exceeding the never-exceed

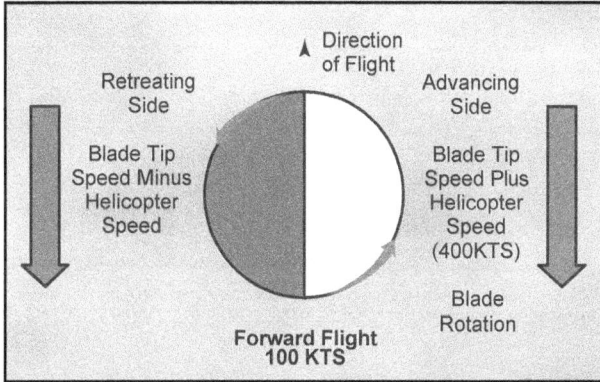

speed. This speed is designated and is usually indicated on a placard and marked on the airspeed indicator by a red line.

During aerodynamic flapping of the rotor blades as they compensate for dissymmetry of lift, the advancing blade achieves maximum up flapping displacement over the nose and maximum down flapping displacement over the tail. This causes the ti path plane to tilt to the rear and is referredtoasblowback.Figure3-16showshowtherotor disc was originally oriented with the front down following the initial cyclic input, but as airspeed is gained and flapping eliminates dissymmetry of lift, the front of the disc comes up, and the back of the disc goes down. This reorientation of the rotor disc changes the direction in which total rotor thrust acts so that the helicopter's for- ward speed slows, but can be corrected with cyclic input. Drag now acts forward with the lift component straight up and weight straight down.

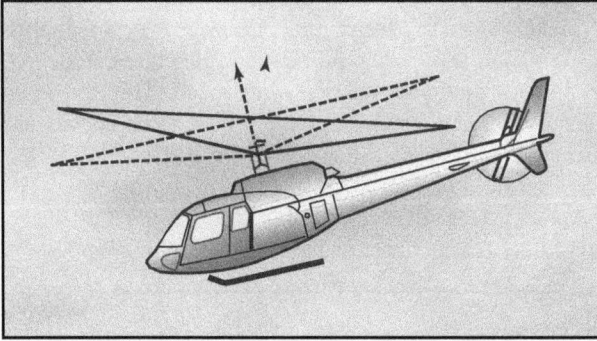

SIDEWARD FLIGHT

In side ward flight, the tip path plane is tilted in the direction that flight is desired. This tilts the total lift-thrust vector sideward. In this case, the vertical or lift component is still straight up and weight straight down, but the horizontal or thrust component now acts side ward with drag acting to the opposite side.

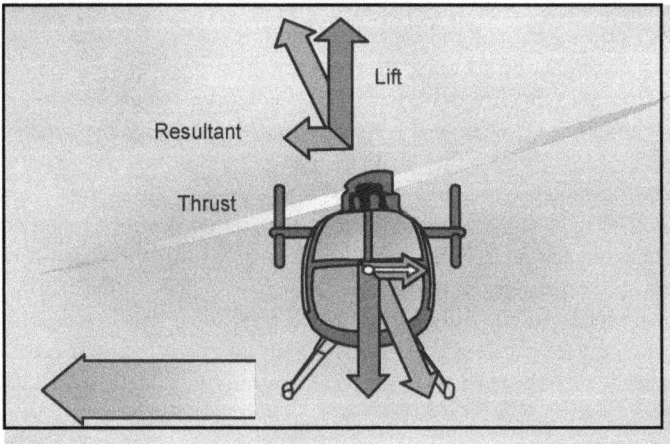

REARWARD FLIGHT

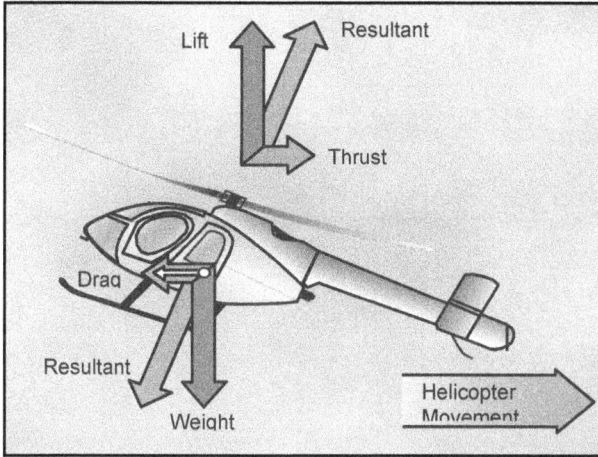

For rearward flight, the tip-path plane is tilted rear- ward, which, in turn, tilts the lift-thrust vector rear-

TURNING FLIGHT

In forward flight, the rotor disc is tilted forward, which also tilts the total lift-thrust force of the rotor disc for- ward. When the helicopter is banked, the rotor disc is tilted side ward resulting in lift being separated into two components. Lift acting upward and opposing weight is called the vertical component of lift. Lift acting horizontally and opposing inertia (centrifugal force) is the horizontal component of lift **(centripetal force)**

As the angle of bank increases, the total lift force is tilted more toward the horizontal, thus causing the rate of turn to increase because more lift is acting horizon tally. Since the resultant lifting force acts more horizontally, the effect of lift acting vertically is deceased. To compensate for this decreased vertical lift, the angle of attack of the rotor blades must be increased in order to maintain altitude. The steeper the angle of bank, the greater the angle of attack of the rotor blades required to maintain altitude. Thus, with an increase in bank and a greater angle of attack, the resultant lifting force increases and the rate of turn is faster.

AUTOROTATION

Autorotation is the state of flight where the main rotor system is being turned by the action of relative wind

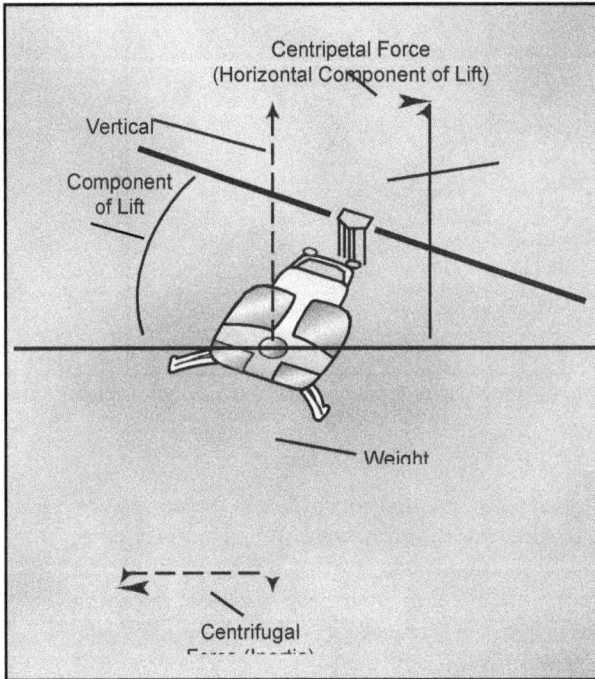

Continue turning even if the engine is not running. In normal powered flight, air is drawn into the main rotor system from above and exhausted downward. During autorotation, airflow enters the rotor disc from below as the helicopter descends.

AUTOROTATION (VERTICAL FLIGHT)

Most auto rotations are performed with forward speed. For simplicity, the following aerodynamic explanation is based on a vertical auto rotative descent (no forward speed) in still air. Under these conditions, the forces that cause the blades to turn are similar for all blades regardless of their position in the plane of rotation. Therefore, dissymmetry of lift resulting from helicopter airspeed is not a factor.

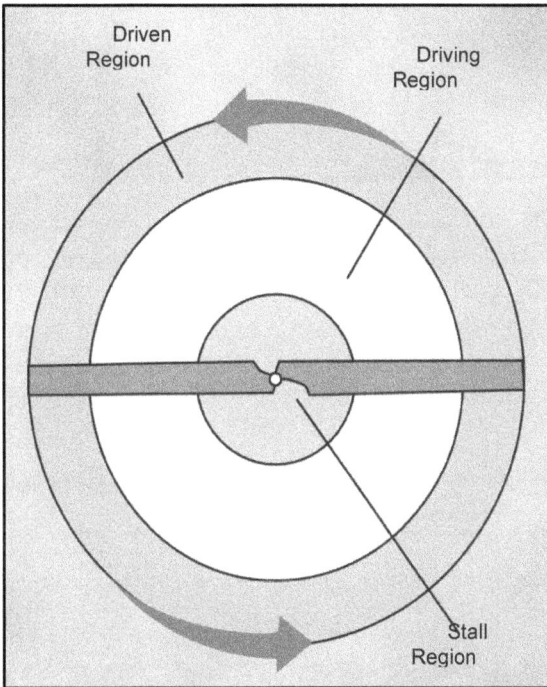

During vertical autorotation, the rotor disc is divided into three regions as illustrated in the

rather than engine power. It is the means by which a helicopter can be landed safely in the event of an engine failure. In this case, you are using altitude as potential energy and converting it to kinetic energy during the descent and touchdown. All helicopters must have this capability in order to be certified. Autorotation is permitted mechanically because of a freewheeling unit, which allows the main rotor to con-driven region, the driving region, and the stall region.

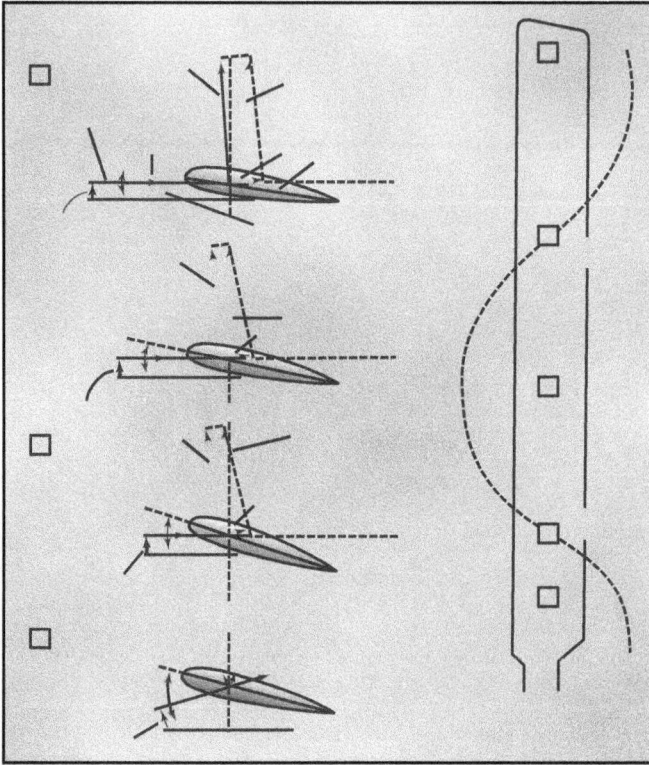

Four blade sections that illustrate force vectors. Part A is the driven region, B and D are points of equilibrium, part C is the driving region, and part E is the stall region. Force vectors are different in each region because rotational relative wind is slower near the blade root and increases continually toward the blade tip. Also, blade twist gives a more positive angle of attack in the driving region than in the driven region. The combination of the inflow up through the rotor with rotational relative wind produces different combinations of aerodynamic force at every point along the blade.

Percent of the radius. In the driven region, part A of, the total aerodynamic force acts behind the axis of rotation, resulting in a overall drag force. The driven region produces some lift, but that lift is offset by drag. The overall result is a deceleration in the rotation of the blade. The size of this region varies with the blade pitch, rate of descent, and rotor R.P.M. When changing autorotative R.P.M., blade pitch, or rate of descent, the size of the driven region in relation to the other regions also changes.

There are two points of equilibrium on the blade—one between the driven region and the driving region, and one between the driving region and the stall region. At points of equilibrium, total aerodynamic force is aligned with the axis of rotation. Lift and drag are produced, but the total effect produces neither acceleration nor deceleration.

The driving region, or autorotative region, normally lies between 25 to 70 percent of the blade radius. Part C of figure 3-22 shows the driving region of the blade, which produces the forces needed to turn the blades during autorotation. Total aerodynamic force in the driving region is inclined slightly forward of the axis of rotation, producing a continual acceleration force. This inclination supplies thrust, which tends to accelerate the rotation of the blade. Driving region size varies with blade pitch setting , rate of descent, and rotor R.P.M.

By controlling the size of this region you can adjust autorotative R.P.M. For example, if the collective pitch is raised, the pitch angle increases in all regions. This causes the point of equilibrium to move inboard along the blade's span, thus increasing the size of the driven region. The stall region also becomes larger while the driving region becomes smaller. Reducing the size of the driving region causes the acceleration force of the driving region and R.P.M. to decrease.

The inner 25 percent of the rotor blade is referred to as the stall region and operates above its maximum angle of attack (stall angle) causing drag which tends to slow rotation of the blade. Part E of depicts the stall region. A constant rotor R.P.M. is achieved by adjusting the collective pitch so blade acceleration forces from the driving region are balanced with the deceleration forces from the driven and stall regions.

AUTOROTATION (FORWARD FLIGHT)

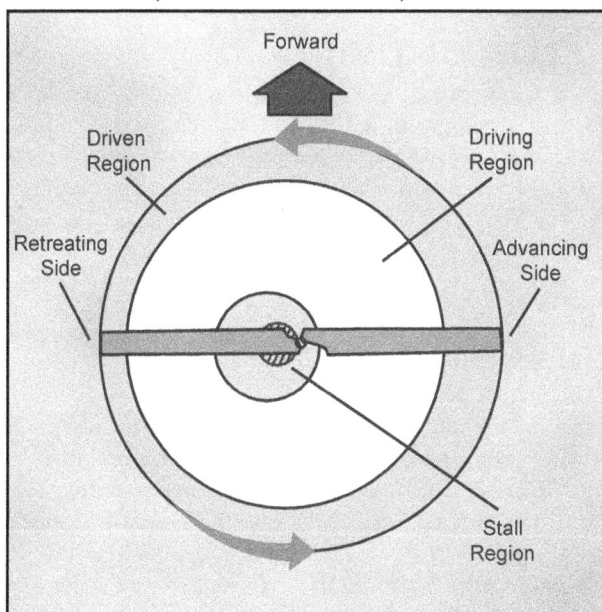

Autorotative force in forward flight is produced in exactly the same manner as when the helicopter is descending vertically in still air. However, because forward speed changes the inflow of air up through the rotor disc, all three regions move outboard along the blade span on the retreating side of the disc where angle of attack is larger, as shown in. With lower angles of attack on the advancing side blade, more of that blade falls in the driven region. On the retreating side, more of the blade is in the stall region. A small section near the root experiences are versed flow, therefore the size of the driven region on the retreating side is reduced. simultaneously, or collectively, as the name implies. As the collective pitch control is raised, there is a simultaneous and equal increase in pitch angle of all main rotor blades; as it is lowered, there is a simultaneous and equal decrease in pitch angle. This is done through a series of mechanical linkages and the amount of movement in the collective lever determines the amount of blade pitch change. An adjustable friction control helps prevent inadvertent collective pitch movement.

Changing the pitch angle on the blades changes the angle of attack on each blade. With a change in angle of attack comes a change in drag, which affects the speed or R.P.M. of the main rotor. As the pitch angle increases, angle of attack increases, drag increases, and rotor R.P.M. decreases. Decreasing pitch angle decreases both angle of attack and drag, while rotor R.P.M. increases. In order to maintain a constant rotor R.P.M., which is essential in helicopter operations, a proportionate change in power is required to compensate for the change in drag. This is accomplished with the throttle control or a correlate governor, which automatically adjusts engine power.

THROTTLE CONTROL

The function of the throttle is to regulate engine R.P.M. If the correlator or governor system does not maintain the desired R.P.M. when the collective is raised or lowered, or if those systems are not installed, the throttle has to be moved manually with the twist grip in order to maintain R.P.M. Twisting the throttle outboard increases R.P.M.; twisting it inboard decreases R.P.M.

COLLECTIVE PITCH / THROTTLE COORDINATION

When the collective pitch is raised, the load on the engine is increased in order to maintain desired R.P.M. The load is measured by a manifold pressure gauge in piston helicopters or by a torque gauge in turbine helicopters. In piston helicopters, the collective pitch is the primary control for manifold pressure, and the throttle is the primary control for R.P.M. However, the collective pitch control also influences R.P.M., and the throttle also influences manifold pressure; therefore, each is considered to be a secondary control of the other's function. Both the tachometer (R.P.M. indicator) and the manifold pressure gauge must be analyzed to determine which control to use. illustrates this relationship.

CORRELATOR / GOVERNOR

A correlator is a mechanical connection between the collective lever and the engine throttle. When the collective lever is raised, power is automatically increased and when lowered, power is decreased. This system maintains R.P.M. close to the desired value, but still requires adjustment of the throttle for fine tuning.

A governor is a sensing device that senses rotor and engine R.P.M. and makes the necessary adjustments in order to keep rotor R.P.M. constant. In normal operations, once the rotor R.P.M. is set, the governor keeps the R.P.M. constant, and there is no need to make any throttle adjustments. Governors are common on all turbine helicopters and used on some piston powered helicopters.

Some helicopters do not have correlators or governors and require coordination of all collective and throttle movements. When the collective is raised, the throttle must be increased; when the collective is lowered, the throttle must be decreased. As with any air craft control, large adjustments of either collective pitch or throttle should be avoided. All corrections should be made through the use of smooth pressure.

CYCLIC PITCHCONTROL

The cyclic pitch control tilts the main rotor disc by changing the pitch angle of the rotor blades in their cycle of rotation. When the main rotor disc is tilted, the horizontal component of lift moves the helicopter in the direction of tilt. The rotor disc tilts in the direction that pressure is applied to the cyclic pitch control. If the cyclic is moved forward, the rotor disc tilts forward; if the cyclic is moved aft, the disc tilts aft, and so on. Because the rotor disc acts like a gyro, the mechanical linkages for the cyclic control rods are rigged in such a way that they decrease the pitch angle of the rotor blade approximately 90° before it reaches the direction of cyclic displacement, and increase the pitch angle of the rotor blade approximately 90° after it passes the direction of displacement. An increase in pitch angle increases angle of attack; a decrease in pitch angle decreases angle of attack. For example, if the cyclic is moved forward, the angle of attack decreases as the rotor blade passes the right side of the helicopter and increases on the left side. This results in maximum downward deflection of the rotor blade in front of the helicopter and maximum upward deflection behind it, causing the rotor disc to tilt forward.

HEADING CONTROL

Besides counteracting torque of the main rotor, the tail rotor is also used to control the heading of the helicopter while hovering or when making hovering turns. Hovering turns are commonly referred to as "pedal turns."

In forward flight, the anti torque pedals are not used to control the heading of the helicopter, except during portions of crosswind takeoffs and approaches. Instead they are used to compensate for torque to put the helicopter in longitudinal trim so that coordinated flight can be maintained. The cyclic control is used to change heading by making a turn to the desire direction.

The thrust of the tail rotor depends on the pitch angle of the tail rotor blades. This pitch angle can be positive, negative, or zero. A positive pitch angle tends to move the tail to the right. A negative pitch angle moves the tail to the left, while no thrust is produced with a zero pitch angle.

With the right pedal moved forward of the neutral position, the tail rotor either has a negative pitch angle or a small positive pitch angle. The farther it is forward, the larger the negative pitch angle. The nearer it is to neutral, the more positive the pitch angle, and somewhere in between, it has a zero pitch angle. As the left pedal is moved forward of the neutral position, the positive pitch angle of the tail rotor increases until it becomes maximum with full forward displacement of the left pedal.

If the tail rotor has a negative pitch angle, tail rotor thrust is working in the same direction as the torque of the main rotor. With a small positive pitch angle, the tail rotor does not produce sufficient thrust to overcome the torque effect of the main rotor during cruise flight. Therefore, if the right pedal is displaced forward of neutral during cruising flight, the tail rotor thrust does not overcome the torque effect, and the nose yaws to the right.

With the anti torque pedals in the neutral position, the tail rotor has a medium positive pitch angle. In medium positive pitch, the tail rotor thrust approximately equals the torque of the main rotor during cruise flight, so the helicopter maintains a constant heading in level flight.

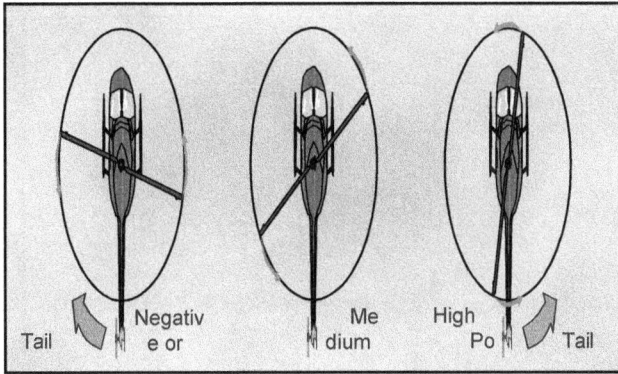

If the left pedal is in a forward position, the tail rotor has a high positive pitch position. In this position, tail rotor thrust exceeds the thrust needed to overcome torque effect during cruising flight so the helicopter yaws to the left.

The above explanation is based on cruise power and air- speed. Since the amount of torque is dependent on the amount of engine power being supplied to the main rotor, the relative positions of the pedals required to counteract torque depend upon the amount of power being used at any time. In general, the less power being used, the greater the requirement for forward displacement of the right pedal; the greater the power, the greater the forward displacement of the left pedal.

MAIN ROTOR SYSTEM

Main rotor systems are classified according to how the main rotor blades move relative to the main rotor hub. As was described in Introduction to the Helicopter, there are three basic classifications: fully articulated, semi rigid, or rigid. Some modern rotor systems use a combination of these types.

FULLY ARTICULATED ROTOR SYSTEM

In a fully articulated rotor system, each rotor blade is attached to the rotor hub through a series of hinges, which allow the blade to move independently of the others. These rotor systems usually have three or more blades.

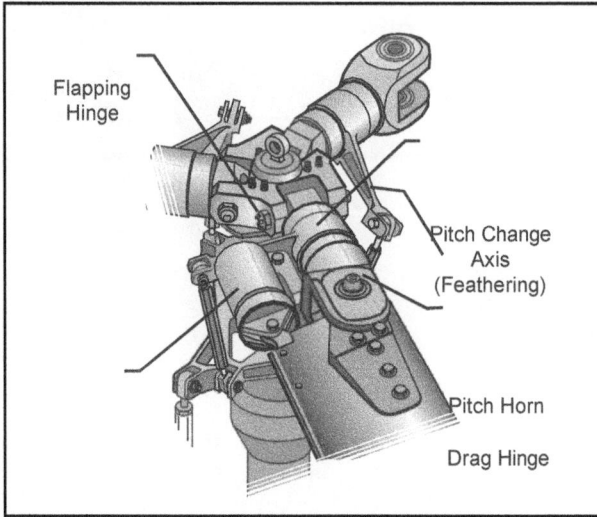

The horizontal hinge, called the flapping hinge, allows the blade to move up and down. This movement is called flapping and is designed to compensate for dis-symetry of lift. The flapping hinge may be located at varying distances from the rotor hub, and there may be more than one hinge. The vertical hinge, called the lead-lag or drag hinge, allows the blade to move back and forth. This movement is called lead-lag, dragging, or hunting. Dampers are usually used to prevent excess back and forth movement around the drag hinge. The purpose of the drag hinge and dampers is to compensate for the acceleration and deceleration caused by Coriolis Effect. Each blade can also be feathered, that is, rotated around its span wise axis. Feathering the blade means changing the pitch angle of the blade. By changing the pitch angle of the blades you can control the thrust and direction of the main rotor disc.

SEMIRIGID ROTOR SYSTEM

A semi rigid rotor system is usually composed of two blades which are rigidly mounted to the main rotor hub. The main rotor hub is free to tilt with respect to the main rotor shaft on what is known as a teetering hinge. This allows the blades to flap together as a unit. As one blade flaps up, the other flaps down. Since there is no vertical drag hinge, lead-lag forces are absorbed through blade bending.